I0804206

Light and DARKNESS

Essential Biblical Perspectives on African Traditional Religion

Richard J. Gehman

OASIS INTERNATIONAL PUBLISHING

Light and Darkness: Essential Biblical Perspectives on African Traditional Religion

Copyright © 2024 by Richard J. Gehman

All rights reserved. No part of this publication may be reproduced, distributed, or transmitted in any form or by any means, or stored in any database or a retrieval system without prior written permission of the publisher. The only exception is brief quotations in books or critical reviews.

ISBN 13: 978-1-59452-808-8
ISBN 10: 1-59452-808-X

Published by Oasis International Ltd. in partnership with Richard J. Gehman.

Oasis International is a ministry devoted to growing discipleship through publishing African voices.

- We ***engage*** Africa's most influential, most relevant, and best communicators for the sake of the gospel.
- We ***cultivate*** local and global partnerships in order to publish and distribute high-quality books and Bibles.
- We ***create*** contextual content that meets the specific needs of Africa, has the power to transform individuals and societies, and gives the church in Africa a global voice.

Oasis is: Satisfying *Africa's Thirst for God's Word.* For more information, go to oasisinternational.com.

The author and publisher have made every effort to ensure that the information in this book was correct at press time and disclaim any liability to any party for any loss, damage, or disruption caused by errors or omissions, whether such errors or omissions result from negligence, accident, or any other cause. However, if you feel that your work was not accurately cited, please reach out to us at info@oasisinternational.com and we will make every effort to review and correct the book where required. Furthermore, any internet addresses (websites, blogs, etc.), telephone numbers, or the like in this book are offered only as a resource. They are not intended in any way to be or imply an endorsement by Oasis, nor does Oasis vouch for this content.

All Scripture quotations, unless otherwise indicated are taken from the *Holy Bible*, New Living Translation, copyright © 1996, 2004, 2007, 2015 by Tyndale House Foundation; Anglicized Text Version, © SPCK 2018. Used by permission of Tyndale House Publishers Inc., Carol Stream, Illinois 60188, USA, and SPCK, London, UK. All rights reserved.

Scripture quotations marked ESV are taken from the ESV® Bible (The Holy Bible, English Standard Version®), Anglicized English Standard Version copyright® 2002 by Crossway and HarperCollins Publishers, London. Used by permission. All rights reserved.

Scripture quotations marked NIV are from the Holy Bible, New International Version® Anglicized, NIV® Copyright © 1979, 1984, 2011 by Biblica, Inc.™ Used by permission. All rights reserved worldwide.

Scripture quotations marked Phillips are taken from The New Testament in Modern English by J. B. Phillips copyright © 1960, 1972 J. B. Phillips. Administered by The Archbishops' Council of the Church of England. Used by permission.

Printed in India.

24 25 26 27 28 29 30 31 32 33 BPI 10 9 8 7 6 5 4 3 2 1

A Note from the Editor

"We don't typically discuss this outside of our circles, especially not with a non-African," my friend said softly.

I was stunned. Honoured that she felt safe sharing with me, but stunned because doing so could be considered taboo.

"But it is so important!" she continued. "We need to be doing more to help Christians in Africa understand the way traditional religion is impacting their faith and their families."

My friend told of a recent situation where a prominent family member expected her husband to participate in a traditional ceremony in support of a family marriage event. Her husband was uncomfortable with the ceremony, so they dug into God's Word together, sharing what they found with the prominent family member who is also a Christian.

"What happens if we don't participate?" my friend and her husband respectfully asked their family member. "Bad things will happen. You'll be blocking family blessings," was the response. Ultimately my friend and her husband chose not to participate in the traditional ceremony because of their faith convictions based on what they studied in God's Word, but they intentionally found other ways to support their family. It was not enough. By not participating, a rift developed in their family that took time to heal.

Many religious practices worldwide are often so deeply woven into the culture of families, tribes, villages, and nations, that it can be hard to determine the path of holiness. It is not a case of throwing away all tradition to follow a western version of Christianity as some have mistakenly attempted. Nor is it a case of simply blending traditional religions together with Christianity to create new religious paradigms and practices, a practice called *syncretism*.

At Oasis we acknowledge that the topic of African Traditional Religion (ATR) is complex and nuanced. We believe understanding this topic is vital, and one we will continue to engage with respectfully, biblically, and with great care for all our friends across the African continent and throughout the world who are grappling with how to reconcile various cultural traditions with Christianity without diluting the divinity of God and the power of God's Word in our lives.

This book is one voice in the conversation. Dr Gehman, while not of African ethnic descent, has spent a lifetime studying God's Word, living in East Africa, and studying the ways in which ATR is practiced and intersects with Christianity in various African communities. Ultimately, Jesus – the Living Word – has the final say. We invite you to join us in seeking the Living Word for wisdom in all matters.

– Oasis International

Table of Contents

THE SPIRIT WORLD

CONCLUDING THOUGHTS

Preface

Back in 1973 a major turning point occurred in my life. Desmond Hales, the principal of Scott Theological College, asked me to teach a new course on African Traditional Religion (ATR). To prepare for this course, which had never been taught at Scott, he gave me a four-month sabbatical.

With all diligence I scavenged the libraries in Nairobi to photocopy all relevant ethnological and religious studies on the peoples of Africa. From these materials I prepared my teaching notes. For years thereafter I taught ATR more than any other course.

My students helped shape the course as I learned from them their religious heritage. Every term a few students had firsthand experience of ATR. They enriched the discussion. Amazingly, there were also a few students who knew virtually nothing of ATR since they grew up in Christian homes. Most students had a secondhand knowledge. More than once they nailed me to the wall for sentiments expressed that were offensive. From all these interactions the course curriculum was shaped.

When the college revised the curriculum for the Bachelor of Theology degree, I arranged to teach ATR in two terms. The first term of three credit hours focused on the general beliefs and practices of ATR throughout Africa. Before sending students off to do primary research during their one-month holiday, I taught them some basic principles of field research. The second term of two credit hours was devoted to student class presentations of their primary research written in substantial research papers. Their work was spectacular!

After several years I wrote a 150-page book on ATR which a kind, good Samaritan in the United States offered to type on mimeographing stencils. This book was used in several Bible schools of the Africa Inland Church.

In 1980 I began work on a Doctor of Missiology and chose to write my dissertation on ATR, entitled: *Ancestor Relations among Three African Societies in Biblical Perspective.* For this I did further field and library research, graduating in 1985. The final version of the dissertation was 649 pages long after they eliminated three chapters.

By 1989 I self-published a 310-page textbook entitled, *African Traditional Religion in Biblical Perspective.* A free copy was sent to every Bible school and college in Anglophone Africa. As a result, thousands of copies were ordered, sent in bundles of five books, to every corner in Africa, from South Africa to Ethiopia, from Ghana to Kenya. After several years the East African Educational Publishers became the publisher with a fully revised edition of 410 pages published in 2005. Oasis International took over the publishing in 2012.

African Traditional Religion in Biblical Perspective is a carefully researched book with 10 pages of bibliography and hundreds upon hundreds of bibliographical notations. A simplified version of this book, *African Traditional Religion in the Light of the Bible* is published by Africa Christian Textbooks for Nigeria.

What has happened with this labour of love is a demonstration of what God can do with very little. In all candour, I was never a pioneer missionary nor the master of any African mother tongue. But God gave to me an inquisitive mind, a sensitive spirit, and a learning heart. By God's grace he has been pleased to use that book to provide a biblical perspective on ATR.

One day when studying in the Wheaton College Graduate School library an African walked swiftly across the room to greet me. To my astonishment he had studied ATR in Ghana by using my textbook. "I used to ask my fellow students," he said, "Who is this Gehman? He knows more about ATR than we do!" Amazing! To God alone be the glory.

This present book, *Light and Darkness: Essential Biblical Perspectives on African Traditional Religion*, is a summary of the textbook compacted in less than 130 pages. It is designed for people who desire to learn the basic outline of biblical teaching concerning the traditional beliefs and practices in Africa.

The study begins with a foundational statement of the biblical perspective for understanding ATR. Scholars view traditional religion in Africa with differing presuppositions. The perspective of this book is that God has provided in Scripture the divine revelation by which we interpret all of life.

Our study of ATR is divided into three parts: mystical powers, the spirit world, and the supreme being. In each of these parts we study traditional African beliefs and practices, followed by a survey of similar beliefs held throughout the world. The basic ATR beliefs of mystical powers, spirits and divinities, and the supreme being are found throughout the world. Finally, and most importantly, we examine the biblical teaching.

Through the lens of Scripture, we understand the truth and error in ATR, knowing that God "has not left himself without testimony" (Acts 14:17, NIV), "so that people are without excuse" (Romans 1:20, NIV). Yet those same people "suppress the truth" and their "foolish hearts [are] darkened" (Romans 1:18, 21, NIV).

OVERVIEW OF CULTURE AND AFRICAN TRADITIONAL RELIGION

1

Biblical Perspective

This book is not a simple description of African traditional beliefs and practices in the 19th century. It is an attempt to understand and interpret African Traditional Religion today in the light of biblical teaching.

AFRICAN TRADITIONAL CULTURE

African *religion* was always integrated within African culture. In fact, there is generally no indigenous word for *religion*. So, what is culture?

What Is Culture?

We may say that culture is "a total plan for living," "a way of life of a particular social group" that is learned from infancy and is integrated into a "functionally organised system".[1] Culture is all learned behaviour and a unique way of understanding the world. Culture includes material objects, patterns of learned behaviour, beliefs, and values.

Material Objects

Culture includes material objects such as housing, clothing, dishes and utensils, ways of communication, entertainment, education, and objects used in governing society. This aspect of culture is relatively easy to change as we can all see. Today much of Africa is quite modern with cell phones, classrooms filled with chairs, desks and chalkboard, TV, and cinema as forms of entertainment, and the use of a Parliament Building with a mace, wigs, and robes.

Beliefs

But culture at a deeper level (a world view) is very difficult to change. A world view is a way of understanding and interpreting the world around you. It includes *beliefs* – belief in the Creator God, divinities, nature spirits, ancestral spirits, and mystical powers of magic, witchcraft, and sorcery. Beliefs include causes of sickness and death, health and prosperity, and the need for divination to determine the causes of misfortune. Beliefs provide an explanation for everything that happens.

Values

This deeper level of a world view includes *values* which consists of a sense of what is right or wrong, moral or immoral, proper or improper. Beliefs and values persist because they are learned from infancy and are unexamined. They seem normal and natural, logical, and reasonable. Besides, everyone else believes and follows this traditional world view.

Because all men and women are made in the image of God, we find much good in all cultures. But because human beings are fallen creatures who do not love God with all their hearts and obey him completely, we find much evil in all cultures. Culture A may be better than culture B in certain areas, but in other ways culture A is deficient compared to culture B.

Evaluating Culture

The premise on which this book is written is that the Christian Scriptures are the standard by which we judge right and wrong, good and evil, acceptable and unacceptable. The Bible was not written by the will of humans but by the prophets and apostles who were "carried along by the Holy Spirit" (2 Peter 1:21, NIV). "All Scripture is breathed out by God . . ." (2 Timothy 3:16, ESV). Jesus taught that God's Word is "truth" (John 17:17). Moreover, "not an iota, not a dot, will pass from the Law until all is accomplished" (Matthew 5:18, ESV).

It is true that western missionaries assumed that some of their western values were biblical values and taught them to Africans as biblical values. Now that a growing and maturing African church has been planted, African believers no longer need to rely on what missionaries taught them. They can and should rely wholly and entirely on what the Scriptures teach.

When Paul preached the Good News that Jesus was the Christ (Messiah), many Jews and Gentiles believed, but the majority of the Jews became jealous in unbelief and began using violence to attack Paul.

He then fled to the neighbouring town of Berea where he continued to preach the gospel. We read that "these Jews were more noble than those in

Thessalonica; they received the word with all eagerness, examining the Scriptures daily to see if these things were so" (Acts 17:11, ESV).

Following is my understanding of a biblical world view through which we evaluate African Traditional Religion. It is filled with biblical references. My prayer is that people who read this book will not simply believe and accept what is written. Instead, they will study the Scriptures for themselves and follow the example of the Bereans who examined (studied) the Scriptures "to see if these things were so."

A healthy, growing church anywhere in the world is a biblically literate church. Every Christian should read the Scriptures from Genesis to Revelation repeatedly. It is easy to pluck a verse out of context to support your view. We must understand the biblical text within the immediate context and the broader context of Scripture. God has provided a unique resource for Africa in the *Africa Study Bible*. Buy, read, and meditate on it.

A BIBLICAL WORLD VIEW

A biblical world view will enable us to understand and interpret ATR in the light of the Bible. No attempt will be made to present a comprehensive world view from Scripture. Three basic elements in a biblical world view will be explored in this chapter: the God of creation, the nature of human beings, and the triumph of the gospel.

The God of Creation

Our view of God profoundly affects our world view. We mimic those whom we adore. Our standard of behaviour grows out of our beliefs in God. As the Bible teaches, "Be holy, for I am holy" (Leviticus 11:44-45, ESV). The Lord God of creation is matchless in his splendour and glory.

- *Intellectually,* God is all-knowing and all-wise in everything he does.
- *Ethically,* God is holy, righteous, true, just, merciful, gracious, loving, and faithful towards all his creatures.
- *Emotionally,* God loves and is patient with all sinners, but detests evil.
- *Volitionally,* God is sovereign, free, and omnipotent in everything he chooses to do.

- *Relationally,* the transcendent Divine Being is immanent universally in providential activity and immanent with his people in redemptive activity.[2]

The Three-in-One God

Essential to a Christian world view and held by the Christian church from the beginning, is the biblical teaching that there is only one true and living God (Deuteronomy 6:4f; 1 Corinthians 8:6), but God is *triune*, or three-in-one. God is one in essence, nature, substance, and being as well as one in power, glory, and eternity. Within the Godhead there are three Persons – God the Father, God the Son, and God the Holy Spirit – eternally equal in power and glory and worthy of worship. Each Person has different roles in the plan of salvation.[3]

Maker of Heaven and Earth

God is the creator of all things: the earth and the universe (Genesis 1:1), man and woman in God's image (Genesis 1:26-27), angelic beings – *all things* visible and invisible, physical, and spiritual (Colossians 1:16).

The Nature of Human Beings

The human condition is the same worldwide. Whether in Europe, Asia, Africa, or the Americas, human beings have the same human nature of good and evil. "From one man he [God] made all the nations, that they should inhabit the whole earth" (Acts 17:26, NIV).

Created in the Image of God

All human beings have descended from Adam and Eve, made in the likeness of God (Genesis 1:26f). The Creator God is not an impersonal power but a personal Being with *intellect* who thinks and knows. He expresses *emotions* of joy, sadness, and anger, and has *a will* to choose and decide. Adam and Eve were likewise persons with intellect, emotions, and a will who reflected God's glorious moral nature of *holiness* – righteous, loving, truthful, and just. As God's vice-regents, God endowed our first parents with the *ability and mandate to rule* over the earth.

Fallen in Sin

The descendants of Adam and Eve, however, are no longer *good.* Adam and Eve lost their good nature by defiantly rebelling against the will of God (Genesis 3).

"Therefore, just as sin entered the world through one man, and death through sin, and in this way death came to all people, because all sinned" (Romans 5:12, NIV). Human nature has been substantially altered. Men and women are spiritually dead in transgressions and sins (Ephesians 2:1). They do evil because their human natures are sinful, not only because of negative, evil influences in society (Romans 3:23).

Our condition is worse than most people imagine. It is not just that we are full of greed, selfishness, envy, hatred, strife, lust, and deceit. Our worst predicament is that our hearts are idol factories as John Calvin famously said. There are so many things we elevate above God – ourselves, our spouses, jobs, wealth, pleasure, and more. When people turn from the worship of the only true and living God, they create gods for themselves beginning with their own self-glorification. Human hearts are continually creating gods to whom they devote their time, affection, and loyalties.

Idolatry is essentially the worship of the creature and created things in the place of the Creator God. No human being apart from God's grace can obey the greatest commandment: "Love the Lord your God with all your heart and with all your soul and with all your mind" (Matthew 22:37, NIV). Whoever does not obey that command perfectly (and *no one* does), is an idolater. He exalts his own will and suppresses God's will (Romans 1:18-23).

Idolatry may involve the worship of images of wood, stone, and precious metals, or it may be the veneration given to objects of nature – the sun, moon, and stars (Psalm 135:15-18; Isaiah 44:9-20). Central to idolatry is the proud human being who exalts himself and his own will and desires above the will of the Creator.

Dual Dispositions

Because of these two facts of human nature (created in the image of God and spiritually dead in transgressions and sins), human beings exhibit dual dispositions. Wherever you turn, in whatever part of the world you may be, you will find people who are loving, kind, helpful, and altruistic, and at the same time they are mean, nasty, greedy, and selfish.

Whether people are Muslims, Hindus, Buddhists, Christians, Animists, or followers of African Traditional Religion, we find people who are both kind and generous as well as selfish and proud.

General Revelation and Common Grace

Despite God's displeasure at man's disobedience, God has graciously restrained his wrath by revealing himself to all peoples everywhere through nature and conscience. God has revealed his invisible attributes of power and glory through what is visible in nature (Romans 1:20). The vast expanse of the universe and the order of creation reveals that some Intelligent Being greater than feeble human beings has created the universe (Psalm 8:1f; 19:1f).

Furthermore, everyone has a conscience, an inner voice that commends or condemns for deeds done. Every person has a sense of right and wrong which should lead people to repent and turn to God (Romans 2:12-16). For God "is patient towards you, not wishing that any should perish, but that all should reach repentance" (2 Peter 3:9, ESV).

The great church theologian of African descent, Augustine of Hippo, born in AD 354 in present today Algeria, made this remarkable observation: "Because you have made us for yourself, and [therefore] our hearts are restless till they find their rest in Thee."[4] God created human beings for a personal relationship with him. Because people are alienated from God, human beings are restless until that personal relationship is restored. They lack meaning, purpose, and fulfilment in life. By common grace people intuitively realise something is missing in their lives.

Through common grace we find the preservation of some sense of truth, morality, and goodness among all the peoples. Even though the truth is suppressed it cannot be obliterated. We find people feeling guilty for sin and an emptiness in their soul. Without common grace humanity would be living in hell-like conditions even while on earth.

The Triumph of the Gospel

From what has been said to this point, it is clear that the primary problem in our world today is sin against God and not the consequences of sin. Because of sin people live in fear of enemies who may bewitch them, fear of spirits who may destroy their prosperity and health, fear of drought and famine, fear of war and violence, and fear of sickness and death. *Fear!*

But God in his mercy has made known to us in the Scriptures his holy love and grace. Therein we read the whole story of redemption from the first creation (Genesis, first book of the Bible) to the final creation of a new heaven and new earth (Revelation, last book of the Bible).

God the Father has graciously sent his only Son, the Lord Jesus Christ, to die on the cross as the sacrificial Lamb of God. Through repentance of sin and faith in Jesus Christ, sinful men and women are born again and adopted into God's family as children of God (John 3:16; Romans 3:21-26).

No religion, including cultural Christianity, can save a person from God's judgement on sinful human beings. No religion can provide peace with God and rest for the soul. Only a personal faith in Jesus Christ gives eternal life.

In view of this foundational perspective, we approach our biblical study of African Traditional Religion. ATR reflects both God's gracious revelation in conscience and nature which leads to noble practices in African experiences. It also reflects the deadness and darkness of human nature as ATR reflects the factories of idolatry in human hearts.

Our Final Authority in Faith and Conduct

The Bible is God's revelation in propositions, infallible and inerrant, verbally inspired by the Holy Spirit, and the supreme and final authority of faith and conduct. God's final and greatest revelation is in the Person of Jesus Christ about whom we know through the Scriptures.

The Christian church throughout history has gone astray whenever they have strayed from the clear teaching of Scripture and have held on to church traditions instead. With God's help we seek to be faithful to Scripture in this book, but as we all know, our perspectives are limited and sometimes erroneous. We need the Holy Spirit and one another across cultural boundaries to arrive at a fuller understanding of the truth.

2

Holistic World View of African Traditional Religion

ATR EMBRACES ALL OF LIFE

Religion in Africa was not a separate category of culture like the economy or governance. Religion permeated all of culture and therefore we describe it as *holistic*. African religion permeates all of life. Most African mother tongues have no word for *religion*. Unlike western culture since the days of the Enlightenment, African culture cannot be divided into sacred and secular. All of culture is sacred.

MAN-CENTRED RELIGION

ATR centres on man in concrete situations. Religion is not abstract theology. It is the practice of Africans worshipping and practicing their beliefs, and these beliefs focus on the good life of Africans. ATR centres on man's interests and needs. John Mbiti describes ATR as *anthropocentric*.

> African philosophy is basically anthropocentric: man is at the very centre of existence, and African peoples see everything else in its relation to the central position of man. God is the explanation of man's origin and sustenance; it is as if God exists for the sake of man. The spirits are ontologically in the mode of between God and man; they describe or explain the destiny of man after physical life . . . Animals, plants, land, rain and other natural objects and phenomena, describe man's environment, and African peoples incorporate this environment into their deeply religious perception of the universe.[5]

NATURE OF HUMAN BEINGS

Africans believe that human beings are both material and immaterial, tangible and intangible, body and spirit, though some African beliefs can be complex in their views of the spirit. Unlike evolutionary teaching of the west, Africans believe that humans are distinct and different from animals.

Africans have traditionally believed that a living person is filled with energy, a life force, a vital principle. The equivalent in English is *soul* or *spirit*. The presence or absence of this spiritual energy is known by the fact that the person is alive or dead. The absence of *breath* indicates the departure of this spiritual element.

LIFE IN RELATIONSHIPS

Unlike modern western emphasis on individualism, Africans have traditionally stressed living in community. Human relationships are a priority. Africans are related together in families, clans, and tribes. As John Mbiti commented: "I am, because we are, and since we are, therefore I am."[6] This emphasis on relationships is one of the strongest elements in African culture and reflects Hebrew Old Testament culture.

Modern industrialization, urbanization, education, and transportation are inevitably breaking down close-knit communities of Africa just as it has done in the West.

Orphanages were unknown in traditional Africa for the extended family cared for the orphans. Modern education is breaking down traditional values and relationships. The elders are no longer viewed as the bastions of wisdom. Women are no longer dependent on husbands for support.

A traditional African family is extended beyond the nuclear family of the West (father, mother, and immediate children).

Most African languages have no separate word for brothers/sisters and cousins. All cousins in western terms are brothers and sisters in Africa. Neither is there a separate word for mother/father and aunts/uncles. The traditional African has many fathers and mothers. Relationships between aunts and uncles are just as close as with the biological parents.

The extended family extends to the grandparents and even the deceased ancestors. Most traditional Africans believed that relationships with dead ancestors continued for generations after their death until their memory was forgotten. The living seek guidance from their dead ancestors through mediums and show honour to them through offerings and sacrifices. On their part the ancestors appear to them in dreams and show displeasure through sickness, death, accidents, or famine. When ancestral traditions are maintained, the ancestors will reciprocate by granting a good harvest with health and wealth. When the traditions are neglected, the ancestors retaliate.

For the traditional African families to succeed and prosper they needed many children who could herd the cattle, care for the animals, and work in the fields. The size of the families, however, would be of no value without unity. Unity was essential. If one person became a loner and failed to contribute his part, the disunity would offend the ancestors and result in tragedy. Because of this, great effort was made to maintain the traditions, customs, and morals to avoid punishment by the aggrieved ancestors. Traditional rituals and ceremonies were believed necessary to maintain peace and equilibrium in society.

GROWTH IN LIFE CYCLES

The African concept of time is cyclical like most other cultures untouched by Christianity. Life begins with birth and proceeds to puberty, marriage, having children, and death. This is repeated in endless cycles, generation after generation.

It is a natural way of looking at life. But Christian teaching changed this perspective. Oscar Cullman noted that the *line* represents the biblical concept of time, whereas most cultures, including the Greeks, represented time with a *circle* (an endless cycle of events).[7]

From the Christian point of view, history begins with the creation of the heavens and earth, continues through generations of redemptive history (present), and culminates when Jesus Christ returns (future). Through the influence of Christianity all western cultures, touched by the gospel, view time as a line, not a circle.

Occupational Cycle

Agricultural life centres on the weather cycle: rain and drought. When the rains failed, extraordinary ceremonies were practiced, including child sacrifice in some cases, to appease the spirits and bring forth the rain. Rituals may be performed over the implements used in cultivating. The seed sown may be kept in an ancestor shrine or blessed in some way. Taboos may be practiced during the growing season.

Similar dependency on the spiritual realm usually accompanied the hunters and gatherers.

Life Cycle

Similar dependency on the realm of the spirits occurred throughout the cycle of life: birth, initiation, marriage, and death. African societies are highly structured with increased honour accorded to successive stages. Transitions from one stage to another are marked with ceremonies and these are all religious in nature.

Birth

Birth is most important because without the birth of many children, the future well-being of the family and clan is imperilled. Birth is also a dangerous moment in family life because of the infant mortality rate. Because of the importance and potential peril of birth, this cycle of life is surrounded by religious activities. Usually, the ancestors are invoked, and taboos are practiced to placate the departed.

Initiation

Puberty marks the transition from childhood to adulthood. Many African communities mark this event with circumcision, though religion may not be so obvious. Anthropologist Myrtle Langley studied the Nandi life crisis rituals and concluded that religion played no role. But through the insistence of Christian informants, she discovered that religious symbols and appeals to God occurred frequently throughout Nandi rituals.[8]

Marriage

Marriage and the birth of children are central to all life in Africa. Unmarried men or women are unthinkable in traditional African society. Anthropologists often treat African marriage as a mere social event and fail to see the religious implications. Marriage in Africa implies procreation and wherever there is procreation of new life, there are ancestors. Strict traditions from the ancestors are passed down, generation after generation, which must be followed to receive blessing and not trouble from the ancestors.

Death

More rituals are performed at death than during any other rite of passage because death is a portent of extreme danger. Apart from old people, death is always thought to be caused by external forces. Therefore, death is followed by investigation into the cause of death, whether by witchcraft, sorcery, or an evil eye. Death disrupts the peaceful balance prevailing in the world. Therefore, care is taken to restore the equilibrium by various rituals varying among the peoples.

CONCLUSION

Because the invisible world interpenetrates the visible, the traditional African uses all spiritual powers at his disposal during transitions in life, including mystical powers of magic, witchcraft, and sorcery, as well as their relationship with departed ancestors.

MYSTICAL POWERS

3

Mystical Powers in African Tradition

In the words of John Mbiti, "The whole psychic atmosphere of African village life is filled with belief in this mystical power. African peoples know that the universe has a power, or force or whatever else one may call it."[9]

Exactly what this mystical power is cannot be explained, though every traditional African knows it is real. Found in all corners of Africa and among all peoples, this mystical power explains success and failure.

> Life force is vital for health, wealth, worldly power, and success – in fact, everything that makes life at all worth living. To have it is to be healthy and strong; to lose it is to grow weak and die. It exists in greater concentration in famous men, strong charms, revered fetishes, and powerful gods. Gods, humans (both living and departed), animals, and plants have life only as they have this vital force.[10]

Nothing occurs by accident in life. Everything has a cause beyond the natural, observable world. Explanation for events is rooted either in spirit beings, benevolent or malevolent, or in impersonal mystical powers which animate the living. When some Africans feel tired and exhausted, they reply, "I am dying." By this they mean that their decrease of vital powers, if left unchecked, will lead to death.

These mystical powers are manifested in magic, divination, witchcraft, and sorcery.

MAGIC

Magic is the manipulation of mystical powers by using rituals consisting of words and actions to help or harm others. Africans are not ignorant of natural causes and effects, but believe in the spiritual aspect of life, a spiritual world beyond the material that interacts with the material world.

Good magic, also known by Africans as *white magic*, protects and helps. Protection from injury and harm is achieved by using charms and amulets worn by the person; by the chanting of a magic formula; and the use of herbs, seeds, powder, skins, and feathers by a skilled practitioner such as a diviner, magician, or witch doctor.

Whereas good magic is favoured by the peoples and practiced openly in the day, *bad magic*, also known by Africans as *black magic*, is practiced secretly at night because people disapprove of it. Black magic is used to harm and destroy others and their property out of revenge or jealousy. John Mbiti asserts: "A great deal of belief here is based on, or derives from fear, suspicion, jealousies, ignorance, or false accusations, which go on in African villages."[11]

Magic may be for personal or public use. Charms may be worn by individuals to protect from evil forces. Or magical rituals may be performed to enhance one's performance, such as improving one's harvest or gaining favour of the opposite sex.

Magic may also be used by the family and community. Houses may be protected by hanging charms over the doorway or placed in the roof. Fields may be protected from malevolent attacks by burying in the fields charms made of a packet with bones, feathers, sticks, skins, or leaves.

Magic appears to be based on one of two principles: *like produces like* and *things once in contact continue to act on each other at a distance.*

Things that look alike (*like produces like*) have effect on each other. A common example of this is the use of an effigy, a model of the person intended for harm. By inserting thorns into the effigy and hitting it, the same afflictions will be felt by the person targeted. In times of drought the diviner may spit water into the air to imitate the falling of rain. The medicine man may plaster spots on the body of a sick person, then wash them away, imitating the removal of sickness.

Things once in contact continue to act on each other at a distance, sometimes called *contagious magic*, is quite common. Hair, fingernails, clothes, and faeces are used in black magic to harm the person from whom the items were once in contact. It is common for women to preserve the placenta and umbilical cord of the baby lest it be used to harm the baby.

DIVINATION

Strange and undesirable events occur in life such as a drought, accidents, or a barren wife. How do we explain them? Secular westerners usually explain them away by saying it was bad luck or good luck, just chance. The African world view sees beyond the physical world. There is always a reason, a personal and intelligent reason, behind the strange and unusual events in this visible world.

To learn the reason behind the tragedy, the traditional African consulted with the diviner. This specialist uses extraordinary means to discover the cause of the disaster or to inform the best way forward. To *divine* is simply the effort to foresee the future or to discover the reasons behind the strange and unusual events.

Divination may involve the interpretation of different kinds of items. A diviner may throw a bunch of objects on the ground and then interpret the meaning by examining the pattern or configuration of the pieces. He may examine the entrails of an animal, or the footprint found in ashes and find meaning in the lines or shapes before him. Or a common man may interpret the flight formation of birds or their chirping.

Diviners may serve as mediums who consult the spirit world to divine an explanation of the events. Through dreams and visions, the spirits may communicate to the diviner. Or he may use drugs and herbs to induce a trance whereby the spirits communicate through the diviner.

WITCHCRAFT AND SORCERY

Much confusion has occurred in the use of the English words *witchcraft* and *sorcery*, so it is imperative to distinguish them at the outset. Evans-Pritchard, a recognised authority on the subject, said:

> The chief difference between a sorcerer and a witch is that the former [sorcerer] uses the technique of magic and derives his power from medicines, while the latter [witch] acts without rites and spells and uses hereditary psycho-physical powers

> to attain his [or her] ends. Both alike are enemies of men. . . . Witchcraft and sorcery are opposed to, and opposed by, magic.[12]

There is a great variety and diversity among Africans in their beliefs of witchcraft and sorcery. Usually, Africans themselves do not distinguish between witchcraft and sorcery. Nevertheless, it is helpful to understand that the power behind these mystical powers is of two kinds: one uses *medicines*, usually poison, and the other uses psychical/spiritual powers.

Sorcery and Black Magic

A sorcerer always uses medicines to obtain his purposes. Most commonly the sorcerer derives his power through the use of poison. Hence a sorcerer is a black magician using black magic.

When Jomo Kenyatta describes the Gikuyu, he speaks of a *witch* and *witchcraft*. However, in fact, what he describes is sorcery. The Gikuyu word for witchcraft is *orogi*, meaning *poison* and the one who uses the poison is a witch, *morogi*. And Kenyatta claims that "*orogi* is pure and simple poison."[13]

Witch and Witchcraft

The powers of a witch are inherent in the person. Witches are usually female, though not all. They are eccentric or deformed or behave contrary to the norms in society. They are said to be evil in themselves and perform wicked deeds because of their wicked natures and thus they are feared.

Witch doctors are specialists who treat people who are bewitched. Because of the negative connotations of the name, many prefer calling them *medicine-men* or *witch-finders*. These specialists may also serve as diviners, rainmakers, or priests.

Witches are feared and perform their work in secret. Witch doctors are *highly respected*, though feared, and perform their work in the open during the day. They are seen as public servants fighting witchcraft.

However, it is important to understand that witch doctors use the same powers as the witches. *Vital force* that is found in people, animals, trees, plants, and inanimate objects is neutral; it is neither good nor bad. Witches usually use this *vital force* for evil but can use it to improve crops and reverse the evil spells they have made. By the same token, witch doctors generally use this power for healing or protection, but they can also use their power to attack others.

CONCLUSION

Mystical powers permeated all of traditional African life. Magic, divination, witchcraft, and sorcery were the focal point of African beliefs and practices and maintain a stubborn foothold in modern African societies, even as they did in western nations after their Christianization.

The life force or vital energy, which permeates everything in degrees, is a neutral power which can be used positively to help or negatively to harm.

4

Mystical Powers Worldwide

Africa is not unique in its beliefs and practices of mystical powers. Magic, divination, witchcraft, and sorcery are practiced worldwide in folk religions which in turn have infiltrated the major world religions.

ANCIENT HISTORY

Written magic spells intended to ward off witches were found in ancient Egypt and Mesopotamia around 4000 BC. Magic abounded in Greek mythology with the use of amulets. Anglo-Saxons in England used a rabbit's foot for a charm, and Germanic and Nordic literature claimed that dragon's blood could provide protection.

The pseudo-science of predicting the future by examining the movement of the stars can be traced to 3000 BC in Mesopotamia. Examining the liver to divine the future was common in the mid-eastern world. In 1000 BC China was known to have divined the future from the cracks in scorched shoulder blades. Nearly all peoples in the world have believed that the movement of birds or beasts had special meaning. Diviners in Rome used mechanical means such as the throwing of pebbles.

WORLD RELIGIONS

Islam allegedly began with Muhammad crusading in the seventh century against the idolatry in Arabia. But much of Islam practiced worldwide today is better known as Folk Islam because the peoples have absorbed their former traditional beliefs in mystical powers found in folk religion. By Africanizing Islam, Africans have more readily become Muslims.

Magic is very prominent in Folk Islam by integrating traditional beliefs into Islam. For example, Islam in Africa teaches that by reading properly Surah

2:256 in the Quran, all your needs are supplied. Or by closing the fists in both hands then reading Surah Al-Fatihah (Surah 1) 10 times and removing one finger from the closed hand in reverse order after each reading, all your needs are met if done for 40 days correctly. The Quran is not read for its meaning, but for magical purposes.

Amulets incorporate the names of Allah for magic and sorcery. Traditional belief in spirits is transformed into *jinn*. The alleged relics of Muhammad including his hair, teeth, and footprints are powerful magic.

CONTEMPORARY WESTERN BELIEF IN MYSTICAL POWERS

Tens of thousands of westerners engage in the *occult*, which means *hidden things*. Techniques used by New Age specialists to learn *hidden* things include meditation, chanting, mood-altering music, mind-expanding drugs, religious mysticism, hypnosis, and more.

Astrology is rooted in ancient paganism and appeals to modern man as scientific, though in fact it is a pseudo-science. It is believed that the movement and location of the planets influence people and events. Horoscopes are used by astrologists for this purpose. Thousands of newspapers carry daily horoscope columns. Astrological predictions are available through astrological computer calculators and paperback guides.

Channelling is used to obtain revelation of hidden knowledge. This involves a *medium*, also called a *channeller*, who goes into a trance to reveal hidden mysteries from *the other side*.

Geoffrey Parrinder has studied witchcraft, comparing Africa with the western practices 200 years ago.[14] Similar characteristics include:

1. *Animal familiars*: witches were associated with various animals, most commonly black cats. It was said that witches can turn themselves into one of these animal familiars.
2. *Night flying*: it was thought that witches could ride at nighttime on animal familiars. While the body remains asleep, the spirit escapes and wanders about at night.
3. *Eating human flesh*: witches were accused of killing and eating unbaptised children. To curtail these activities 200 hundred years ago,

> Americans and Europeans hunted alleged witches, killing an estimated 300,000 people.

Today there is a surprising movement of *neopaganism*. Thousands of people in Europe and America call themselves *pagans* or *neopagans* and witches. They believe in gods and the *primordial realm* above the gods. Satanism exists with thousands of people[15] killed in satanic rituals.

CONCLUSION

Africans have shared with all members of humanity a belief in mystical powers to explain life's fortunes and failures and to seek refuge in their power. Today, Africa is importing from western countries such occult practices as astrology, reading of horoscopes, and satanism.

5

Mystical Powers in Biblical Perspective

INTERPRETATION OF MYSTICAL POWERS

The dominant theme in African Traditional Religion is mystical powers – the powers of magic, divination, witchcraft, and sorcery. By these powers they explain sickness and death, the central concerns of the peoples. They also have the staying power many years after African communities have embraced Christianity. These mystical powers seem real, so how should we understand them?

ATR Perspective

We could simply agree uncritically with the view of traditional Africans. Whatever they believe, we also believe: that mystical powers are from vital energy that pervades most everything in various measures. However, many western scholars disagree.

Naturalistic Perspective

Most scholars of African Traditional Religion embrace a naturalistic, rationalistic interpretation. Most anthropologists and psychologists deny the existence of supernatural occult powers or unseen spirit activities, even Africans who have studied under western naturalistic professors.

Biblical Perspective

From a biblical perspective, we discover a remarkably balanced view of ATR. It does not dismiss Africans as superstitious as many westerners have done, even missionaries.

I vividly recall attending the Ngelani Africa Inland Church in Ukambani, Kenya, where the highly respected pastor, whom missionaries had trained well, declared from the pulpit that witchcraft was superstition. Amid the sermon a woman stood up and repudiated this claim, stating that from her experience she knew that witchcraft was not superstition but reality.

In the early years of teaching ATR at Scott Theological College, I was sceptical of many accounts of mystical realities. They seemed wild and imaginary, rather unbelievable. But the more I interacted with students the more I was compelled to take the reality of these accounts seriously.

On one hand the Bible recognises the reality of magical powers. The Egyptian magicians were able to perform miracles similar to those produced by Moses (Exodus 7:11, 22; 8:7, 18f). God did not dismiss Egyptian magic as superstition; rather, the superior power of God was demonstrated by defeating the magicians of Egypt. The same was true with the Babylonian magicians (Daniel 1:20; 2:2, 27; 4:7, 9; 5:11). The authority of the Antichrist will be confirmed by miracles (2 Thessalonians 2:9-12; Revelation 13:13-18). However, the power to do extraordinary feats is not derived from some impersonal vital force, but from evil spirits.

On the other hand, both biblical teaching and African testimony confirm that specialists often do cheat and deceive people with their tricks. They are so deceitful that traditional Africans do not always trust them and seek advice from several witch doctors who live at a distance to confirm or deny the findings of the first one consulted. Other people believe that witch doctors are liars whose only ambition is to acquire wealth.

Moreover, people can be self-deluded. They can be blinded by sin and so persuaded by their own beliefs that they confuse their dreams for reality. Many witches and sorcerers in ninth-century Europe made public claims of leaving their bodies at night and flying on animals to distant places. The Christian church has recognised this self-delusion. The Council of Ancyra in the ninth-century stated:

> Some wicked women, reverting to Satan, and seduced by the illusions and phantasms of demons, believe and profess that they ride at night with Diana on certain beasts . . . Therefore, priests everywhere should preach that they know this to be false and that such phantasms are sent by the Evil Spirit who deludes them in dreams.[16]

Years later this decree, known as *canon Episcopi*, branded *night-flying* to be *illusory* and became part of the canon law of the Catholic Church.

Conclusion

It is extremely difficult to pass judgement on particular cases, whether they are truly miraculous or the result of trickery or self-delusion. But we firmly believe that mystical powers claimed by traditional Africans are not always illusion by a superstitious people.

Montague Summers wrote a classic on European witchcraft. He concluded that when every allowance is made and every possible explanation exhausted, "a mass of solid proven facts" cannot be adequately accounted for by medical or psychological knowledge, "save by acknowledging the reality of witchcraft and diabolic contracts."[17]

BIBLICAL TEACHING ON MYSTICAL POWERS

Numerous scholars seek to incorporate certain mystical powers into their Christian faith. Vincent Mulago, a Roman Catholic priest, believes that apart from black magic and sorcery, African mystical powers should be "cherished as a black African religious synthesis" when purged of errors.[18]

This combining of religious beliefs is contrary to the teachings of Scripture. We discuss that further in the final chapter of this book. However, a careful reading of the Bible reveals that mystical powers are uniformly condemned by God, both in the Old Testament and the New Testament.

Old Testament

The most comprehensive passage in the Bible which prohibits mystical powers is in Deuteronomy. It includes all the Hebrew words for the occult.

> When you enter the land the Lord your God is giving you, be very careful not to imitate the detestable customs of the nations living there. For example, never sacrifice your son or daughter as a burnt offering. And do not let your people practice fortune-telling [divination], or use sorcery, or interpret omens, or engage in witchcraft, or cast spells [magic], or function as mediums or psychics, or call forth the spirits of the dead [necromancy].

> Anyone who does these things is detestable to the Lord. It is because the other nations have done these detestable things that the Lord your God will drive them out ahead of you. But you must be blameless before the Lord your God. The nations you are about to displace consult sorcerers and fortune-tellers, but the Lord your God forbids you to do such things (Deuteronomy 18:9-14).

Because of the sins of the nations recorded in Genesis 1–11, God brought judgement on the world's population through the worldwide Flood, and on the people building the Tower of Babel.

Therefore, God chose Abraham and his descendants, the nation of Israel, to bless the nations through Christ (Genesis 12:1-3). As the Lord said: "Of all the people on earth, the Lord your God has chosen you to be his own special treasure" (Deuteronomy 7:6b). Therefore, God warned Israel not to imitate the practices of the nations.

Human Sacrifice

In Deuteronomy 18:10, the Hebrew phrase for human sacrifice can be translated literally: "passing one's son or daughter through the fire." We do not know how this was done, but we know the nations living in the Promised Land offered their children as sacrifices in desperate prayers to their gods. Though human sacrifice was formerly practiced in Africa during desperate times of famine, no one today would publicly condone or practice such abominations.

Divination

Fortune telling (i.e., *divination*) is the art of acquiring hidden knowledge of the future by supernatural means. This usually requires consultation with a diviner. All ancient societies sought such hidden knowledge when faced with a crisis. This was true of the Canaanites who consulted the specialists who dealt with the powers of darkness.

Israel, however, was forbidden the use of occult powers to predict the future. As the Lord's special people, Israel was commanded to trust God alone. All astrologers were scorned by the prophet Isaiah (Isaiah 47:13-14).

Three kinds of divination were used by the neighbouring Semites as mentioned in Ezekiel 21:21. "He shakes the arrows, he consults the teraphim [household idols], he looks at the liver" (ESV).

Examining the liver was an ancient practice. After a sheep was slaughtered, the diviner examined the markings of the liver to determine the answer to the question asked. Divination by arrows involved placing marked arrows in a quiver. After shaking and casting out the arrows, the first arrow that came out gave the answer.

Another means of divining was *interpreting omens.* Down through the ages people have imagined various things to be good or bad omens. Both the *Septuagint* (Greek translation of the Old Testament) and the *Latin Vulgate* translation interpret the general Hebrew word for *omen* by the Greek and Latin word for *omens from birds.* The flights of birds were thought to observe the thoughts of humans below and portend the future with good luck or bad luck. Birds assumed the role of divinity, knowing hidden things and revealing the future.[19]

Any form of divination is forbidden by God according to Scripture. "You shall not interpret omens or tell fortunes" (Leviticus 19:26, ESV). "Do not let your people . . . interpret omens" (Deuteronomy 18:10). Divination and interpreting omens were among the great sins of King Manasseh which brought final judgement on Israel (2 Kings 21:6, 11-15).

Why does God pronounce such strong opposition to all divination? What is wrong with seeking advice from diviners to avert danger or tragedy? Who wouldn't want to learn of a future event or learn what course of action to take? Isn't that helpful? Shouldn't divination be an innocent practice that Christians could cherish, like the Roman Catholic priest, Vincent Mulago, recommends?

Not according to the Scriptures! Divination is strictly rejected in Scripture because God is opposed to the powers of darkness. People who consult diviners are traitors to their Lord and Saviour. A spiritual battle is taking place, and God's people are called to pledge total allegiance to God alone.

Leviticus 19 lists an array of practices which God forbids. These include many of the Ten Commandments and commandments forbidding any practices of the occult. The chapter begins with God's command: "You must be holy because I, the Lord your God, am holy" (Leviticus 19:2). These commandments forbidding God's people to practice divination and the interpretation of omens are rooted in God and the identity of God's people. They are made in God's image, saved from bondage to Satan and called to be God's treasured possession for his glory. Forbidding mystical and magical powers are not arbitrary or a mere nuisance. They are rooted in the nature of God's being. Hear the words of the Lord God:

> Thus says the Lord, your Redeemer, who formed you from the womb; "I am the Lord, who made all things, who alone stretched out the heavens, who spread out the earth by myself, who frustrates the signs of liars and makes fools of diviners" (Isaiah 44:24-25 ESV).

Even if divination is for a *good* purpose and is socially accepted in the community, it is sin and contrary to the will of God to consult with a diviner. Furthermore, it is wrong to trust in the interpretation of omens. This broad condemnation of *interpreting omens* forbids Christians from living under fear that certain omens foretell either a *lucky* day or an *unlucky* time to do something.

What harm is there, one might ask, in cancelling a planned safari because some unlucky omen has been spotted? What harm is there in deciding on a course of action determined in the skies above or the earth beneath? Either such beliefs are mere superstition without any value today, or they have real power because of their participation in the powers of darkness. Judgement is pronounced upon all diviners and people who consult them.

Sorcery

Unlike diviners who practice in the daytime and are socially acceptable, sorcery is practiced at night and is antisocial. The Hebrew word, *kashaph*, used in Deuteronomy 18:10, is translated in the King James (Authorized) Version by the word *witch* and by the New International Version as *witchcraft*. This is most unfortunate. The newer Bible translations use the word *sorcerer*, including the RSV, NASB, ESV, and NEB. The word clearly refers to *black magic* which uses materials such as poison to do harm.

This is in keeping with the recent distinction made between witchcraft and sorcery by anthropologists like Sir Edward Evans-Pritchard, Geoffrey Parrinder, and John Middleton.[20] Witches perform their evil deeds by innate powers without the use of material objects and herbs, whereas sorcerers use materials including poison herbs to do their malevolent deeds. With this distinction in mind, we find no reference in the Bible to witches or witchcraft as defined by these anthropologists.

The very first prohibition against the use of mystical powers in the Mosaic Law occurs in Exodus 22:18. "You must not allow a sorceress to live." One of the works of the flesh is *sorcery* (Galatians 5:20 ESV).[21]

The biblical command is clear: The use of drugs, herbs, or other means to bring about supernatural effects for the harm of other people or the protection of the client is totally forbidden.

Though eastern religions and African Traditional Religion make a distinction between mystical powers that were permitted (divination and white magic) and those rejected (sorcery and black magic), God makes no such distinction. Every occultic practice that seeks to use supernatural means to peer into the future, protect oneself from harm, or to injure others is absolutely, totally, and completely forbidden.

All forms of witchcraft and sorcery are forbidden in Scripture because of their association with demonic activities. Sorcery is associated with practices of spiritualism (2 Kings 23:24), spiritual harlotry (Nahum 3:4), and idolatry (Micah 5:12). The evil of witchcraft is in its dependence upon the creature in defiance of the will of God. That any person would seek help from a wizard rather than God is evidence of demonic idolatry, removing God from his rightful place of pre-eminence (Isaiah 8:19).

Magic

The Mosaic prohibition of magic is expressed literally by the Hebrew word meaning *tie a magic knot.*[22] The Hebrew Lexicon by Gesenius refers this to "a species of magic which was practiced by binding magic knots." In practice a magician would use words or things, such as the tying of knots, to cast a spell.

In contrast to sorcery, which is *black magic*, this mystical power which utilises charms is *white magic*, used for defence against harmful magic. This word is used in the plural in Isaiah 47:9, 12, referring to magic exercised against an enemy in self-defence. It is also used in self-defence against a snake (Psalm 58:5).

Magic is the practice of manipulating supernatural powers to achieve one's desires. Though charms used for self-defence are considered good and socially acceptable in human societies, the use of any magic – *white magic* or *black magic* – is repudiated by God because God desires his children to trust him and not some adversarial spirits.

Scripture recognises the reality of dark powers of evil spirits, but it does not recognise impersonal powers of vital force.

Since all genuine magic is the display of supernatural power, it is personal and the result of living, intelligent spirit beings. Therefore, all such magic is evil before God. For these reasons the practices recorded in Deuteronomy 18 are described as *detestable things*. They are forbidden, not because of some arbitrary will of God, but because they are associated with the adversaries of the Kingdom of God. To participate in them not only reflects unbelief and disobedience, but it also involves the participant in the works of the devil himself.

New Testament

The New Testament is firmly built on the Old Testament. Whatever is taught in the Old Testament is fulfilled and affirmed in the New Testament.

Sorcery

One of the works of the flesh is *sorcery*. Paul wrote forcefully, "Let me tell you again, as I have before, that anyone living that sort of life will not inherit the Kingdom of God" (Galatians 5:21).

Magic

When the gospel was received in Ephesus, the new converts burned their charms and magical potions. The total value was 50,000 pieces of silver, representing a total worth of 50,000 working days (Acts 19:18f). These Christians knew that to be faithful to the Lord Jesus Christ, they needed to sever all connections with the dark powers of the devil.

In like manner the newly converted Africans in the Africa Inland Church in Kenya take their charms and any item associated with witch doctors and publicly burn all such items in a public worship service at the house. The Word of God is preached, prayer is offered, and during the burning process the Christians join in solidarity, singing hymns of praise to God. The new convert participates in collecting the items and casting them into the fire. This marks a total break with everything associated with evil powers.

Every magician is an agent of the devil. His or her ways are detestable in the eyes of God. Elymas, also called Bar-Jesus, was a magician on the island of Cypress. He was rebuked by Paul and called the "son of the devil" and the "enemy of all righteousness" (Acts 13:6-12, ESV). For Christians there is no such thing as *good magic*. If there is any genuine power in charms worn on the body, the power resides in the personal spirits of darkness. Just as likely, those charms are useless, worn by people who are blinded in unbelief.

From the Christian's point of view, the definition of *magic* by *Webster's New Collegiate Dictionary* (1958) is deficient. According to that dictionary, magic is: (1) the art which *claims or is believed* to produce effects by the assistance of supernatural beings or by a mastery of secret forces in nature. . . (2) Hence: *seemingly requiring* more than human power, startling in performance; producing *effects which seem supernatural* (emphasis mine).

Magic can be trickery which people believe is supernatural, but not always. Mystical powers can be real because they are energised and activated by evil spirits.

CONCLUSION

The Bible is clear: All mystical powers are of the devil, even the kind that seem harmless and helpful, including protective charms and any form of divination. For Christians to engage in these practices is a betrayal of the Lord Jesus who saved them. Only the living God can protect, not spirit beings alienated from God. To seek guidance and future knowledge through mystical powers is relying on the creature rather than the Creator. Christians need to make a clear break with mystical powers of all kinds.

6

Theological Solutions to Mystical Powers

Mystical powers still hold influence over many Christians in Africa who resort to diviners for help. They still seek help from ATR specialists. Why should this be? Is the gospel too weak? Are professing Christians not born again?

Paul Hiebert explains this by speaking of a *split-level* Christianity.[23] He visualises reality in three levels: *the highest level* where God lives in the heaven of heavens above; *the lowest level* which we experience on earth with our five senses (see, hear, feel, touch and smell); and *the middle level* which deals with the invisible world of magic, divination, sorcery, witchcraft, ancestral spirits, and divinities.

Dr Hiebert observed that most missionaries preached the gospel and applied it only to *the highest level*: belief in the Triune God, and the gospel which offers forgiveness of sins and eternal salvation through Jesus Christ. *The lower level* was left to the scientists who explain the workings of this natural world. Tragically, these missionaries *excluded the middle level* which dealt with the invisible world of mystical powers and spirits. These powers are thought by African Traditional Religion to be responsible for all tragedies such as accidents, famine, sickness, death, and all other calamities in life. Leaving the middle level unaddressed by the gospel leads many Christians in Africa to seek help from traditional specialists. Whenever tragedy strikes, such Christians resort to traditional remedies of diviners.

Western missionaries were influenced by the world view of their naturalistic culture just as Christians in Africa are influenced by the world view of their traditional culture. Since the Enlightenment of the 17th and 18th centuries, the western world view divides the world into the secular (scientific) and the sacred (religious). Events of this world are explained scientifically, whereas spiritual realities are explained by religion. The gospel of Jesus Christ only applied to eternal salvation.

Biblical Christianity does not make this dichotomy of western scientific thought, but western Christians are easily influenced by this thinking, just as Christians in Africa are influenced by their traditional way of thinking.

What is needed is a recovery of the holistic gospel that applies biblical truth to the whole of reality: the upper, middle, and lower levels.

Scientifically, we understand that many diseases are caused by germs. This is a proven fact. But beyond the material world is the spiritual world which interacts with the material world. This is a biblical truth. Christians need to be taught thoroughly concerning the full work of Christ on the cross, not only providing eternal salvation, but triumphing over the devil with the ability to protect and keep his children. They need to know the sovereignty of God who controls every event in our lives.

Following are biblical truths which should enable Christians to stand strong in their faith and not return to their former beliefs and practices.

A THEOLOGY OF THE SOVEREIGNTY OF THE TRIUNE GOD

ATR is human-centred. The basic characteristic of ATR is "that it tries to make the divine powers an instrument of man's personal welfare".[24] In this world view, African peoples do not seek God for his own sake. They seek him in worship for what they can get out of him.

In contrast the biblical world view is God-centred. God, who revealed himself in the pages of Scripture, is totally and absolutely sovereign over everything visible and invisible. He created the heavens and the earth, all for his glory. He is in control of everything. Nothing happens apart from his divine will. Human beings were created for God's glory. In brief, human beings exist for God's glory. God does not exist for man's benefit, though he blesses people who trust and obey him.

It is true that in African traditional beliefs God is sovereign, but *in practice* he does not exercise his sovereignty in the affairs of human beings. ATR is preoccupied with fear of mystical powers of magic, witchcraft, and sorcery, as well as the spirit world. God is not the primary or usual source of help from those fears. Keith Ferdinando makes this insightful observation:

> The fundamental difference between African and biblical conceptions of the spirit and occult world stems from

> essentially different notions of the Supreme Being. One of the pre-eminent dimensions of the biblical doctrine of God is his universal sovereign government: for the biblical writers the whole cosmos, visible and invisible, is dominated by him, and religious attitudes and practices are shaped accordingly. It is this which is absent from African traditional religion, whose Supreme Beings are not generally understood to exercise such sovereignty . . . Rather, in the living experience of its adherents, it is the world of lesser spirits and of witches and sorcerers which is of dominant spiritual and existential concern. There is a "dependence upon lesser spiritual causalities because there is no adequate recognition that the great power of the one God could really be concerned with this or that side of one's own small life."[25]

The most important ministry every pastor has is to teach and preach and in doing so to teach and preach the majestic beauty of all the attributes of God taught in Scripture including his sovereignty. Instead of preaching against sin all the time, pastors should stress the biblical teaching of all the splendour of God's holiness.

The most important thing a Christian can do is to read, meditate on, and study the Word of God from Genesis to Revelation and learn who God is. This is life transforming. I know because I did this. In a thick notebook I wrote the different attributes of God at the top of each page. As I read the Bible through, beginning in Genesis, I wrote each verse, word for word, which described one of the characteristics of God. This made a tremendous impact on me spiritually. Unless we know God as he has revealed himself in redemptive history, we will fall short in knowing how to live for him. God is wonderful in his power and glory. He is in control. He is good and loves his children. Whenever tragedy comes, God brings this for our good.

Through teaching, preaching, and meditating on the Scriptures, the people of God need to learn through consistent practice to place their full confidence in the sovereign God who is totally in control. Whenever sickness, accident, or death occurs, Christians should not be frightened, because they know that God is Lord of *all*. "I have set the Lord always before me; because he is at my right hand, I shall not be shaken" (Psalm 16:8, ESV). When we know and trust the sovereign Lord, we can be assured that nothing is able to touch us. We rest in his loving, sovereign will. As Paul taught the Roman Christians:

> If God is for us, who can ever be against us? . . . Can anything ever separate us from Christ's love? Does it mean he no longer loves us if we have trouble or calamity, or are persecuted, or hungry, or destitute, or in danger, or threatened with death? . . . No, despite all these things, overwhelming victory is ours through Christ, who loved us (Romans 8:31, 35-37).

A THEOLOGY OF SIN, GRACE, AND SALVATION

The traditional African belief in sin and salvation is radically different from biblical teaching. For traditional Africans the problem in life is the diminishing of the life force, which is evidenced by misfortunes. Tragedies of life such as barrenness, miscarriage of an expectant mother, famine, sickness, or death are material and earthly, causing pain, suffering, and grieving. The cause of these problems is any antisocial act which is aroused by jealousy, hatred, bitterness, or an offense against the living-dead.

With this belief, sin is any act that is antisocial. Salvation, therefore, is doing whatever is necessary to gain acceptance. As Tokunboh Adeyemo writes:

> If any anti-social act is all there is to sin, salvation from sin would be in the same terms. Thus, it is plain in the oral traditions that to be saved primarily means to be accepted. One is first accepted to the community of the living by being good to one's neighbours, and secondly accepted among the community of the dead ancestors by remembering them through libations, prayers, and offerings. An aspect of this acceptance is the struggle for power or *vital force*. It is believed that one who excels his equals has been specially favoured by the ancestors and such an honour is indicative of salvation.[26]

How different is sin and salvation in the Bible! Sin is *disobedience to God and his Word.* Sin is falling short of God's perfect law (Romans 3:23). Salvation cannot be earned by staying on good terms with the community or pleasing the ancestors. Salvation is offered by God as a gift (Ephesians 2:8-9).

Christians should read, meditate on, and even memorise Romans 3:21-26. Understanding salvation from sin is an essential key in finding victory over fear of sickness and death.

A THEOLOGY OF THE CROSS AND THE ASCENDED LORD

The Bible teaches the reality of unseen spiritual powers at work behind the scenes, but this is not impersonal powers as taught by ATR, but personal powers of evil spirits. Since this is true, Christians must understand and believe the gospel concerning the defeat of Satan and his fallen angels by Christ when he died on the cross. Only then will Christians be released from fear of mystical powers, and only then will Christians in Africa no longer feel a need to return to dark powers for healing and protection.

The death of Christ is the pivotal point of human history and the central emphasis of all Scripture. The Bible teaches that Christ died to atone for the sins of humanity. The fundamental problem of humans is not physical but *spiritual*. Humanity's fundamental problem is sinful disobedience of God's law and rebellion against God's will. Deliverance from physical problems of accidents, sickness, and death are not promised in this world, though they are assured for Christians in the world to come when Christ returns.

> You were dead because of your sins and because your sinful nature was not yet cut away. Then God made you alive with Christ, for he forgave all our sins. He cancelled the record of the charges against us and took it away by nailing it to the cross. In this way, he disarmed the spiritual rulers and authorities. He shamed them publicly by his victory over them on the cross (Colossians 2:13-15).

The people in the city of Colossae were spiritually dead without any spiritual life or personal relationship with God. They, like all of us today, were estranged from God, dead in their sins. But Christ made them alive through repentance and faith in Christ who paid for their penalty of sin by his death on the cross in our place. God graciously cancelled (forgave) the record of all the charges against us. This was accomplished on the cross.

Not only did Christ's death on the cross make possible the forgiveness of sins and provide life with God for all eternity; Christ *disarmed* all the evil powers, including Satan and his dominion of evil spirits. These *powers* are the fallen angels with Satan as their leader (Jude 1:6; Revelation 12:8-9). Christ triumphed over them on the cross. Satan and his fallen angels are active but are powerless whenever believers trust Christ to vanquish them.

I love to sing that little chorus: "Under the blood of Jesus, safe in the Shepherd's fold. Under the blood of Jesus, safe while the ages roll. Safe though the worlds may crumble, safe though the stars grow dim. Under the blood of Jesus, I am secure in him."[27]

This truth should be a real comfort for all believers. We need not fear the evil hosts for the battle has been won. God has *disarmed* them when Christ died on the cross. Christians should prayerfully reflect on this truth by reading the Scripture so they can *write* these truths on their hearts. Memorizing the Scripture does wonders. This is a proven means of grace.

God has rescued us from the dominion of darkness (Colossians 1:13). Christ is the head of every principality and authority (Colossians 2:10). These principalities and authorities are creatures, created by Christ (Colossians 1:16). Christ has disarmed all those powers which have opposed his reign (Colossians 2:15). He has bound the strong man (Matthew 12:29).

A BIBLICAL THEOLOGY THAT ADDRESSES THE AFRICAN CONTEXT

The gospel of Jesus Christ is eternally true and relevant to every culture. But it also needs to be applied to the context of every society. The gospel of saving grace is widely preached in Africa with tens of thousands of Africans coming to faith in Jesus Christ. But the gospel has not always been applied to the troubling questions raised by Africans.

A Theology of Sickness, Death, and the Afterlife Is Essential

Christians need to learn to trust in Christ even in times of suffering, sickness, and death, knowing that God has ordained to bring good to us and glory to God through our trials (Romans 8:28).

Believing that God is good all the time, Christians should learn that God has a good purpose whenever bad things happen. As James wrote:

> Dear brothers and sisters, when troubles of any kind come your way, consider it an opportunity for great joy. For you know that when your faith is tested, your endurance has a chance to grow. So let it grow, for when your endurance is fully developed, you will be perfect and complete, needing nothing (James 1:2-4).

We read further the admonition of the apostle Paul:

> We can rejoice, too, when we run into problems and trials, for we know that they help us develop endurance . . . For we know how dearly God loves us, because he has given us the Holy Spirit to fill our heats with his love (Romans 5:3-6).

Notice that *joy* and *rejoicing*, not fear, is the response for Christians when facing trouble of any kind. This is contrary to our usual human reactions. By experience we know that when everything goes well, it is relatively easy to believe in these admonitions. But when trouble strikes, we question, we doubt, and we fear.

A theology of sickness, death, and the afterlife is essential. The secret is genuine, active, practicing faith in the Lord. This faith is grown through prayerfully reading and meditating on the Word of God, and through being tested. "Always be full of joy in the Lord. I say it again – rejoice!" (Philippians 4:4). Our joy is in Christ and his trustworthy promises. Focus on Christ and not on the threatening sea around you, "giving thanks always and for everything to God the Father in the name of our Lord Jesus Christ" (Ephesians 5:20 ESV).

A Theology of Discernment Is Essential

To deny the reality of these mystical powers is unbiblical, but neither is it biblical to be obsessed with evil spirits. Belief in the power of God to heal miraculously is biblical, but an excess focus on physical healing – *believe and receive* – is unbiblical. Many false gospels are being proclaimed and we need biblical discernment. In the name of contextualization many false prophets are rising.[28]

A Theology of Pastoral Care Is Required

Many African believers could be protected from relapse if only their pastors and elders took better care of them, teaching the Word of God as it relates to their fears, visiting them, and praying with them in their homes during times of crises, sickness, suffering, reversals, and death. Theology in the classroom is of little value unless pastors and elders teach it in their churches and practice it in their homes.

CONCLUSION

In many parts of Africa, the fear of witchcraft has not subsided. The tragedy is that in our churches, Bible schools, and colleges the subject of mystical powers is not taught. The full counsel of the Word of God is not taught and applied to these African traditions. Hence, believers are not grounded in their faith.

This is the challenge for the Christian church. The problem is not the deficiency of the Word of God. It is the failure of people entrusted with the responsibility of preaching and teaching the Word of God to equip all believers so that they can stand strong in faith when trials come.

THE SPIRIT WORLD

7

Divinities

Divinities are spirit beings *below* the Supreme Being, said to be ministers of God, and *above* ancestral spirits in their status and power. These divinities are prominent in West Africa and the kingdoms in Uganda but are totally absent from the other portions of Africa.

The complexity of beliefs in these divinities is intensified by the sheer number of divinities. Among the Yoruba, divinities range in number from 401 to 1,700 and are associated with persons, places, and diseases. The Ewe have so many divinities and cults that no comprehensive account is available. In fact, no one knows exactly how many divinities there are among the West Africans.

Some of these gods might be called *nature spirits* because they are personifications of objects in nature such as rivers, lakes, rocks, mountains, and groves of trees. Other divinities are *deified ancestors* who lived and ruled among the peoples in the past. Over time these human beings became elevated to the status of gods. In fact, research has shown that most of the divinities among the Yoruba can be traced back to human beings.

The names and titles given to the Supreme Being among people who believe in divinities suggest that Africans do not confuse divinities with the Creator God. English translations of their titles include *Supreme Creator, God the Chief*, and *the Supreme Protector*. Yet they speak of the divinities as gods.

> Some West African societies regard them as children or messengers of God, while others look upon them as his agents. The divinities may be male or female, good or evil, and are given places of abode or habitats in the environment, such as the hills, rivers, the seas, trees, rocks, and even certain animals.[29]

These beliefs are not coherent or reasoned out in logical fashion. It would be an oversimplification to suggest that a description of divinities can be reduced to a coherent account. Ambiguity abounds in Africa.[30]

THEOLOGICAL PERSPECTIVE

African Scholarly Perspective

Accused of polytheism by Christians and Muslims, numerous African anthropologists and theologians defend ATR as monotheistic. The divinities among the Yoruba have many shrines and priests with active worship, but their Supreme Being has none. To this Noel King replies that the divinities are only attributes, messengers, or agents of the Supreme God.

> The Orisa, then, are the emanations of God's powers, his functioning in certain aspects of his activity as understood by humans. Some are 'personifications' of God's powers in nature, the earth, the rivers, the lagoons, the seas. Some are beings who lived as humans long ago, their divinity recognised later by their descendants. Having 201 or 1,700 Orisa does not make the Yoruba rank polytheists, but simply underlines the wealth of their religious thought.[31]

Kofi Opoku shares the same opinion, believing that divinities are creatures and share the limitations of all other creatures. Their power is limited, not unlimited like God's.[32] Quarcoopomje agrees: "Far from being the object of idolatry the divinities or traditional gods are in a father/son relationship with God. They have derived powers and are functionaries in the theocratic governance of the world."[33]

Bolaji Idowu admits that "the Yoruba appear to be quite satisfied with the divinities with whom they are in immediate touch." But he believes that "once the divinities have been offered their worship, the divinities in their turn will transmit what is necessary of it to Olodumare."[34]

Newell Booth wrestles with the relationship of the Supreme Being and divinities. He admits that it is "extremely complex and confusing". The names for the divinities and Supreme Being "overlap, interpenetrate, and are for some purposes interchangeable". He suggests that the transcendence of God is counterbalanced by the immanence of the divinities.[35]

A Biblical Evaluation

Not all scholars in Africa would agree with the scholars just cited. Cornelius Olowola writes from an evangelical perspective. "To whom is one to pay respect, to the One who sends the message or to the messenger? In order to worship the supreme being, does one have to worship divinities?"[36]

He then affirms: "In the end, the vital issue is not how we prefer to worship, nor whom we prefer to worship, but what God Himself has commanded us to do in His Word. And the Bible leaves no doubt at all on this matter."[37] He concludes: "In biblical perspective, to worship divinities rather than the One God is polytheism, not modified monotheism."[38]

Our standard for interpreting ATR is biblical revelation. How does West African Traditional Religion compare with the biblical world view? With this in mind, we ask several questions.

1. Considering *biblical revelation*, can we believe that the God of Abraham, Isaac, Jacob, and Moses would have anything to do with divination?

   In chapter 5 we saw God's persistent and unrelenting opposition to any form of divination, yet divination is associated with the divinities. The Apostle John admonishes: "Do not believe every spirit, but test the spirits to see whether they are from God." (1 John 4:1, ESV).

   Israel was sold in captivity because, among other things, they "practised divination" (2 Kings 17:17, NIV). Can God ever approve of divinities which are associated with divination?
2. Considering *biblical teaching*, is it possible that "the Lord, whose name is Jealous" (Exodus 34:14, ESV), would tolerate worship devoted to the divinities?

   The worship devoted to divinities is highly developed with many shrines, sacrifices, and worship ceremonies. The main objective of the priests or priestesses is to influence divinities to grant favours. These priestesses are married to the divinities for life and are their servants.

   The Lord God is totally opposed to such idolatrous relationship with any creature. The Lord Almighty declares: "Apart from me there is no God" (Isaiah 44:6, NIV).

   He commands: "You shall have no other gods before (besides) me" (Exodus 20:3, ESV). God demands exclusive worship and will not tolerate any divided loyalty, for God "is a jealous God" (Exodus 34:10-14, ESV).

3. Considering *biblical truth*, can the only true and living God ever accommodate himself to the nature gods of West Africa?

    Many divinities are associated with the powers of nature: thunderstorm, sea, river, and earth. Nature spirits can be appeased and placated to influence the forces of nature.

    But in biblical revelation objects of nature are God's creation and under his control. Judgement fell on the nations that worshipped these nature gods.

    Contrary to the appeals of liberal theologians, Christianity cannot accommodate the divinities of Africa to Africanize Christianity. That would be trying to mix water with oil. Christianity is exclusive.

What is needed is serious biblical study by theologians in Africa who desire to be faithful to the Scriptures, like Yusufu Turaki who declared:

> When man rejected God and his worship, he substituted it with his own man-made divinities, gods and rebellion and worship of creatures or creation instead of God. The African divinities fall in line with the Old Testament definition of man's fall, sin, and rebellion against God. Man rejects absolute worship, service, and obedience to God. Instead, he gives these to his divinities, gods, and spirits he acquires in rebellion against God his Creator.[39]

CONCLUSION

God demands absolute and undiluted loyalty. During her apostasy, Israel did not totally reject the worship of Yahweh; they only wanted to combine the worship of Yahweh with the worship of the Baals, but syncretism led to punishment. We conclude with this challenge given by Olowola

> I must challenge my African brothers and sisters: "How long will you hesitate between two opinions?" . . . Africans worship the divinities and spirits because of their perceived functions, and in order to explain and cope with the

problem of the environment. But in doing so, Africans are worshipping creatures rather than the Creator. Such worship is totally unbiblical and must be considered strictly unacceptable to biblical Christianity on the continent. This matter is not optional and not negotiable. God, and God alone, is to be worshipped and adored.[40]

8

Spirits in African Tradition

Traditionally, Africa was alive with spirits. The Bantu in particular give prominent attention to their ancestral spirits. Jomo Kenyatta, for example, declared that the Gikuyu communed constantly with ancestors.

While true generally of traditional Africans, care must be taken with generalities. Spirits are far less prominent among the Nilotic peoples. Though they believe in spirits, they ignore them and do not fear them. The Murle of South Sudan neither fear them nor seek their favour. They don't even have a word for *spirit possession.*

Hence, this chapter must be understood in light of variation of traditional beliefs. Broadly speaking, there are two kinds of spirits: spirits which have been created by God and ghosts of people who were born as humans.

CREATED SPIRITS

Created spirits are found anywhere and everywhere, especially in remote, unpopulated areas of the bush, forest, rivers, and mountains. Spirits live in birds and animals. For example, if a wild animal meanders into a village, a most unusual thing, Africans will suspect they are indwelled by a spirit.

Some have believed the spirits live beneath the earth, others that the spirits live above the earth in the sky. Spirits possess humans. Wherever spirits may dwell, they are never far from people.

Because these created spirits are unknown and unpredictable, they are greatly feared. These spirits are always attacking, molesting, destroying, and hurting the living. Any tragedy of illness, insanity, or epilepsy may be blamed on them.

ANCESTRAL SPIRITS

Terminology

In the past, scholars writing about African Traditional Religion have referred to these spirits variously as *ancestors, ancestral spirits*, or *dead ancestors*. John Mbiti has objected to these designations and has coined the term, *living-dead*.

He compares the process of dying with the process of living. In life a person moves from physical birth to a naming ceremony, then puberty, initiation, and finally marriage. Even so a person who dies enters the *sasa* (present time frame) with personal immortality, remembered by name, then gradually sinks into the *zamani* (past time frame) when no one remembers him by name. At this point the spirits lose personal immortality and become mere "its" with only corporate immortality.

Although the living-dead are dead physically, they maintain a relationship with people who are alive by communicating through dreams and tragedies. Living people commune with the living-dead by pouring out libations and offerings.[41]

Life after Death

All Africans traditionally believe in life after death. Death is not the end of existence, but the transition into another form of life. Nevertheless, death is feared. No one anticipates the afterlife with joy or hope. People feel a sense of loss even though they believe the living-dead return as ghosts. Life after death is not a desirable existence.

Traditional Africans differ in their beliefs concerning the abode of the living-dead. Many believe they live underground where they were buried. Others believe the living-dead ascend to the sky and live above the earth. Apart from the witches, no distinction among the living-dead is made based on character. There are no rewards or punishments. They all live together in the afterlife.

The afterlife is modelled after this life: boys tend the goats and sheep, women hoe their gardens and reap the crops, men delight in their cattle, and villages are filled with jealousies. Only marriages are missing.

Role of the Living-Dead among the Living

The details of the afterlife are not nearly as important as the interaction of the living-dead with the living. The living-dead serve in various capacities among the living.

1. *As senior elders of the clan, the ancestors function as the guardians of the family traditions and land.* Among the living, age increases respect and authority. The living-dead are the senior elders of the living.
2. *The living-dead correct the errors of the living when they fail to follow the traditions of the fathers.* Traditions and customs must be respected and followed. Any deviance from tradition brings wrath and punishment from the living-dead. Whenever disaster occurs, the diviner is consulted to learn the cause. Often the reason given is the breaking of tradition by the living. Hence, belief in the living-dead hampers innovation, modernization, and change.
3. *The living-dead respond to the requests of the living.* Not only are the many tragedies blamed on the living-dead, but the many blessings of life are attributed to them. The living may beg, request, and ask their ancestors for help. The living implore their ancestors for rain, fertility of the soil, and fertility for their wives.
4. *The living-dead may also serve as intermediaries between man and God.* Being close in time to the living enables the living-dead to best understand the needs of the living. Being closer to God, they have the best channels of communication with the Creator. In African tradition, the living approach the chief through an intermediary closest to the chief. Therefore, the living-dead are reckoned to be the best intermediaries with God.

   However, the fact is that many Africans do not understand that the living-dead are mere intermediaries with God. They assume that the living-dead can themselves answer the prayers of the living. John Mbiti goes beyond the bounds of reason when he insists: "God is the ultimate Recipient whether or not the worshippers are aware of it."[42] When studying ATR, we must learn what the peoples believed and practiced, and not what we as academic scholars think they ought to have believed and practiced.
5. *The living-dead communicate with the living.* They do this through dreams, calamity (to get their attention), diviners (who interpret the meaning of the calamity), possession, and prophets.

OBLIGATIONS OF THE LIVING TO THEIR LIVING-DEAD

Because the living-dead are the senior elders, the living are obligated out of respect and fear to fulfil certain obligations.

- **Obedience.** Throughout life Africans are obligated to obey their elders. How much more are the living expected to obey the mandates of their living-dead! Africans are typically diligent in following ancestral traditions.
- **Communion.** The most common means of communion is through pouring of drink offerings and offering food during the meal. This is the chief way of honouring the dead ancestors.
- **Appeasement.** Ancestors are easily offended and rebuke the living through crisis. The living then appease the ancestors through offerings.
- **Cycle of life and seasons.** Life follows a cycle, marked by ceremonies at birth, naming, initiation, marriage, and death. Seasons are also marked by events: times of rain, planting, and harvest, and times of hunting and fishing. During each cycle the living-dead are remembered and honoured.

ATTITUDES TOWARDS THE LIVING-DEAD

Attitudes toward the living-dead are complex and varied.

- **The living have an ambivalent attitude towards them.** On the one hand, the traditional African feels an affection and respect toward the living-dead who are thought to be their departed family members. On the other hand, the living-dead are feared and dreaded because they remain unseen and are often vindictive and vengeful.
- **The living try to deceive them.** Even though the living-dead are thought to be ever-present with intimate knowledge of the living, the living can deceive them. After the death of several children, a traditional African may name their newborn child, *hyena*, a most

loathsome animal, to deceive the living-dead so that the child will not be snatched from the living.

- **The living scold and mock them.** It is not uncommon for the living to scold, rebuke, threaten, and reprimand the living-dead. Edwin Smith reports this prayer: "You are useless, you gods. You only give us trouble. For although we give you offerings you do not listen to us! You so-and-so are full of hatred. You do not enrich us."[43]

CONCLUSION

Birago Diop, Senegal's poet, pens this haunting poem which describes the relationship of the traditional Africans with their dead ancestors.

> Listen more often to things rather than beings. Hear the fire's voice, Hear the voice of water, In the wind hear the sobbing of the trees. It is our forefathers breathing.
>
> The dead are not gone forever. They are in the paling shadows and in the darkening shadows. The dead are not beneath the ground, They are in the rustling tree, In the murmuring wood, In the still water, in the flowing water, In the lonely place, in the crowd; The dead are not dead.[44]

9

Spirits Worldwide

The basic teachings of ATR can be found in folk religions worldwide. Divinities, gods, and spirits are universal. Traditional relationships with the dead in Africa are neither strange nor novel; communicating with the dead has been found in every continent throughout history. We need to understand ATR in the broader context of religion worldwide.

RELIGIONS OF ANTIQUITY

Ancient Egypt

The cult of the dead focused prominently on the rituals for burying royalty.[45] The living provided the dead king with all that was essential for the afterlife, including clothes, food, boats, small figurines of servants, and more. Magical spells were pronounced to protect the ghost from harm in his wanderings. Offerings were also made by family members to the spirits of the dead who resided in the tombs.

Ancient Persians

Around 800 BC the Persians began following the teachings of Zoroaster. He disapproved of any role of the dead. Yet the Persians continued with their old beliefs in ancestors. They placed meat for the dead in rooms and on the roofs of houses, and burned incense in their honour, for Persians believed that the living and dead were in communion.

RELIGIONS OF THE EUROPEANS

Divinities

The days of the week honour European gods. The sacred day for the Teutons (Germans) was Sunday, honouring the *sun*. They also worshipped the *moon*

(Monday). The oldest Teutonic god was *Ziu* (also transliterated as *Tiu, Tyr* or *Tir*), honoured on Tuesday; *Woden*, the god of war, on Wednesday. The Teutonic god of thunder, rain, and agriculture was *Donor* (or *Thor*), honoured on Thursday. *Frigg*, the Teutonic god of love, is remembered on Friday. The Roman god, *Saturn*, is honoured on Saturday.

Ancestral Spirits

Continued relationships with the dead also prevailed in Europe before the preaching of the gospel. Though not as fully developed by the Romans and Greeks, the basic elements of ancestral veneration were present. Romans believed in life after death and developed practices to propitiate their departed dead and maintain harmonious relationships with them.

Ancestor worship among the Romans included proper burial and annual ceremonies to placate the spirits of the dead. Fear prevailed that unless buried according to tradition, the dead would haunt the living. On several occasions each year festivals were held and offerings given to the dead.

RELIGIONS IN THE EAST

Folk religious beliefs in ancestral spirits persist among major world religions which officially disavow them.

Buddhism

Although Gautama, born 560 BC and later known as Buddha, was humanistic in his thinking with no regard for the spirit world, most Buddhists do not follow classic Buddhism. Fear of spirits is predominant throughout Asia. Placating the spirits dominates the lives of Buddhists.

Confucianism

Confucius, born 551 BC, was a teacher of ethics, not a prophet who taught religious belief in God. He did not deny the supernatural, but never focused on it. Yet intermingling with classical Confucius philosophy are elements of folk religion, including belief in gods, demons, and most prominently ancestor worship.

Islam

Muhammad, born AD 570, became dissatisfied with idolatrous polytheism and the drinking, gambling, and dancing of his fellow Arabs in Mecca. So, he called for the sole worship of Allah, the Creator God. Nevertheless, folk religion has persisted in Islam worldwide. The spread of Islam in Africa was greatly helped by the Africanization of Islam which incorporated African beliefs in evil spirits, ancestral spirits, magic, witchcraft, and charms. Few Africans embrace orthodox Islam but syncretize Islam with African traditional religious beliefs.

CONCLUSION

We conclude that a persistent belief in divinities, gods, ancestors, and mystical powers is found worldwide. People not only believe in immortality of the soul and life after death, but in a continued relationship between the living and the dead. What the living do in this life may either appease the dead or offend them. Mediums are a primary means of communicating with spirits. Much of life is determined by the dictates of the ancestors. In practical terms, the ancestral spirits become a primary focus of the religious belief and practice of mankind. Great effort is made worldwide to appease the dead to avoid attacks from the spirit world. Divinities and lesser gods occupy the devotion of many peoples.

10

Spirits in Biblical Perspective

We have surveyed briefly the traditional African and world beliefs concerning spirits.[46] We now want to examine the biblical teaching concerning spirits so that we can interpret life of the unseen world of spirits in light of God's revelation given to us the Bible.

BIBLICAL PERSPECTIVE OF SPIRITS

Reality and Limitations

Only a biblical world view can approach the traditional African world view with respect because biblical revelation acknowledges the existence of spirits. For the naturalistic westerner, belief in spirits is a sign of ignorance and superstition. Evangelicals accept the reality of spirits because the Bible does.

But peoples around the world who embrace folk religion exaggerate the activity of spirits. The Arabs see demons everywhere in the desert. Because of their vast numbers, certain Arabs must apologise whenever throwing an object, for fear of hitting a spirit. The spirits in Babylon swarmed everywhere, creeping under doors, hiding behind walls, and filling every crevice. The Chinese hear their voices in the strange sounds of the night. In Africa, the Creator God does not control or constrain the work of spirits. As a result, the traditional African sees the activity of the spirits in everything that is unusual and different. Because of this, traditional Africans are in constant fear of spirits.

In contrast, the Bible teaches the reality of spirits within the framework of God's sovereignty. In Scripture God's people do not fear spirits because the living God protects them. Belief in spirits is exaggerated in folk religions, but in Scripture spirits do not dominate all of life.

Demons in the Old Testament

The Old Testament is *theo-centric* (God-centred) because God reigns with all authority over all the earth, including the spirit world.

Satan and Demons

Satan is found by name in only four Old Testament books.[47] He is a personal being who acts as an adversary of God and his people, a liar, and a deceiver.

Demons are only found a few times in the Old Testament. The Hebrew word, *shed*,[48] is used twice for demons as in Psalm 106:36-38. "They worshiped their *idols* . . . They even sacrificed their sons and their daughters to the *demons*. They shed innocent blood, the blood of their sons and daughters. By sacrificing them to the *idols* of Canaan . . ." (emphasis mine). Idols are not lifeless, inanimate objects without power. Worship of idols is animated by demons.

Since God is sovereign and his people are safe in his protection, the Old Testament is not preoccupied with demons like some churches are today.

Ancestral Spirits in the Old Testament

More is said of the spirits of the dead and of mediums in the Old Testament than is said of Satan and demons. Following are a few of the passages that condemn necromancy, the practice of consulting with the dead.

> Do not turn to *mediums* or seek out *spiritists*, for you will be defiled by them (Leviticus 19:31, NIV, emphasis mine).

> I will set my face against anyone who turns to *mediums* and *spiritists* to prostitute themselves by following them (Leviticus 20:6, NIV, emphasis mine).

> A man or woman who is a *medium* or *spiritist* among you must be put to death. You are to stone them (Leviticus 20:27, NIV, emphasis mine).

> When someone tells you to consult *mediums* and *spiritists*, who whisper and mutter, should not a people enquire of their God? (Isaiah 8:19, NIV, emphasis mine).

> The Egyptians will lose heart, and I will bring their plans to nothing; they will consult the idols and *the spirits of the dead*, the *mediums* and the *spiritists* (Isaiah 19:3, NIV, emphasis mine).

Belief in *the possibility of communication* between the dead and the living is universal. The question is: does the Bible support this? The one passage that seems to support this belief is the account of Saul speaking to dead Samuel through the medium of Endor (1 Samuel 28).[49]

A natural reading of 1 Samuel 28 does suggest *necromancy*. Saul wanted to speak to Samuel who had died, and a medium could do this. The truth, however, may be more complex. Three possible explanations are given for the medium of Endor communicating with dead Samuel.

1. The spirit of Samuel *was a deception of the medium*. She was a lawbreaker and could not be trusted. Only she saw the spirit and her description of Samuel was so general it could refer to anyone: "an old man wearing a robe" (28:14, NIV). Saul jumped to the conclusion and *knew* that the spirit was Samuel. We know today that witch doctors deceive the people who trust them. The medium could very well have cheated Saul.

   However, the story of Saul and the medium of Endor does not seem to be a simple account of deception, because the appearance of the spirit frightened the medium (28:12).
2. The spirit of Samuel *was in fact dead Samuel*. Nothing in the account suggests otherwise. However, commentators are divided into two camps: those who believe necromancy was done frequently and those who believe the appearance of Samuel was possible only because of a special working of God. Many find it difficult to believe that an unbelieving medium would be allowed at her discretion to disturb a saint of God in his eternal rest (Philippians 1:21ff). Samuel complained that he was disturbed from his rest (1 Samuel 28:15).

   In other words, mediums are not normally able to disturb the godly who have departed. This account of the medium of Endor genuinely occurred, but it is an exception. No other place in Scripture do we find credence given to necromancy, the living communicating with the dead.

3. The spirit of Samuel *was in fact the devil.* This was the interpretation of the Protestant Reformers as well as numerous early church fathers. For example, Tertullian called the appearance of the spirits, "a rivalry of truth by an unclean spirit." He believed that an evil spirit "represented the soul of Samuel and appeared in the likeness of the prophet . . . We know that Satan himself is transformed into an angel of light – much more into a man of light."[50]

   This interpretation eliminates the problem of God using a practice which he forbade. If necromancy was evil, why would God use such a forbidden practice to disturb God's saint who had departed this life? Something real did happen, which caused the medium to cry "out at the top of her voice" (28:12, NIV). Apart from inferences we have no explicit support for other views.

Dynamic of Apostate Worship

In the biblical world view, demons are associated with the spiritual dynamic that animates worship of other gods. Such worship is not an empty ritual but energised and empowered by the spirit world. As we have seen, the foreign gods are identified with *demons* (Deuteronomy 32:17; Psalm 106:36-38).

Paul cautions the Corinthian believers that, although idols are nothing (1 Corinthians 8:4), demons are the real spiritual entities behind the idols. While idols are lifeless representations of heathen gods, demons are the spiritual powers behind the idols, which inspire and motivate heathen worship (1 Corinthians 10:20). Therefore, Christians should have nothing to do with this worship.

The classic passage that identifies heathen gods with demons is Psalm 96:5: "For all the gods of the nations are idols [demons],[51] but the Lord made the heavens" (NIV). Although these idols are worthless, empty, and vain, behind them is the activity of demons which seek to draw people away from the worship of the Creator God (c.f. Leviticus 17:1-7). There is only one true and living God; any creature that demands worship is empowered by demons.

Demons in the New Testament

Ministry of Jesus Christ

In contrast to the meagre references to demons in the Old Testament, the four Gospels explode with demonic activity during the ministry of Jesus. The Greek word for *demon* occurs 52 times in the Gospels and only eight times in the remainder of the New Testament, including four times in 1 Corinthians 10:20-21.

During his three years of ministry, Jesus preached the Kingdom of God, healed the sick, and cast out demons. By casting out demons Jesus demonstrated his authority over demonic powers. Through Christ's death on the cross, he triumphed over the powers of Satan (Colossians 1:13). By declaring that the Kingdom of God was imminent, Christ confronted Satan and his dominion of darkness. Jesus also gave the apostles "power and authority to drive out all demons and to cure diseases, and he sent them out to proclaim the kingdom of God and to heal those who were ill" (Luke 9:1-2, NIV). Perhaps for these reasons demonic powers became enraged and demonic activity flared up.

From the Gospels we learn the following about evil spirits:

1. They are active spirits who can influence people.
2. They oppose God and all that is good.
3. They are powerful creatures who can oppress people.
4. They can demonise a person.

Ministry and Teaching of the Apostles

The apostles continued the ministry of Jesus after his ascension, heralding God's Kingdom, healing the sick, and exorcising evil spirits (Acts 5:16). But the world of spirits is not a dominant motif outside the Gospels. Only a few references are made to the ministry of exorcism in the Book of Acts (see Acts 16:16-19; 19:12).

Traditional Africans believe intensely in the world of spirits. As Olowola comments: "To deny the existence of these spirits is to deny the existence of African religion."[52] But contrary to ATR and other world religions, the biblical world view is not gripped with fear of spirits. Spirits of all kinds (divinities, evil spirits, and ancestral spirits) are creatures of God who reigns in sovereignty over all of creation. People who are in Christ have every reason to live in peaceful confidence of their security and protection.

BIBLICAL PROHIBITION OF CONTACT WITH SPIRITS

The biblical command is clear: God's people should have absolutely no contact with the spirit world, whether they are ancestral spirits, demons, or familiar spirits. Spirits are neither to be consulted nor implored for guidance or help. No one is permitted to consult people who are mediums with the spirit world. Let's look at the passages.

Deuteronomy 18:10-11

In chapter 5 we examined this passage in the Old Testament that deals comprehensively with the prohibition of pagan practices of mystical powers. We will now consider the remaining practices forbidden, namely, "a medium or spiritist or [one] who consults the dead" (Deuteronomy 18:10-11, NIV).

Medium

Moses declared: "Let no one be found among you . . . who is a medium" (NIV). God detests all practices of communicating with spirits. If a Christian wants to know the will of God for their lives, they are to consult the Word of God given through the prophets (Deuteronomy 18:14-22).

Spiritist

A *spiritist* is defined in the Merriam-Webster dictionary as "a person who claims to speak with or for the *spirits of the dead*" (emphasis mine).[53] Some Bible translations including the Authorized King James Version use the phrase "a consulter with *familiar spirits*" (emphasis mine). There is no essential difference between a spiritist and a medium.

Necromancer

The Authorized King James Version also includes the designation *necromancer*, the only time this word occurs in the AKJV. As we can see from these translations and definitions, there is essentially no difference in meaning between *medium, spiritist,* or *necromancer*. The Bible exhausts the Hebrew vocabulary in Deuteronomy 18:9-14, forbidding all consultation with every spirit, including ancestral spirits.

Isaiah 8:18-20

In the eighth century before Christ, Israel was in a crisis. Pekah of North Israel and Rezin of Damascus wanted Ahaz, king of Judea, to be an ally with them against Assyria. When Ahaz rejected their proposal and preferred friendship with Assyria, Pekah and Rezin joined hands in 734 BC to fight Ahaz, hoping to replace Ahaz with a king agreeable to their plans.

Though God intervened and temporarily saved Judea, terror and fear prevailed among the Jews. When Tiglath-Pileser marched south, overthrowing the king of Samaria and destroying Philistine cities, it appeared as though Judea would fall. In terror, the children of Israel turned to the mediums (the necromancers) to communicate with the spirits of the dead. The prophet Isaiah asked them this question followed by a plea:

> And when they say to you, 'Enquire of the mediums and the necromancers who chirp and mutter,' should not a people enquire of their God? Should they enquire of the dead on behalf of the living? To the teaching and to the testimony! If they will not speak according to this word, it is because they have no dawn (Isaiah 8:19-20, ESV).

How shameful for the people of God to turn to mediums and necromancers for a prophetic word concerning the future. Instead, God commands his people to search "the teaching" and "the testimony" found in the Word of God. For people who reject God and turn toward the dead, God pronounces "distress and darkness, the gloom of anguish" and famine (Isaiah 8:22, ESV).

CONCLUSION

We conclude that God has forbidden all contact of any sort with the spirit world. Communicating with the dead is spiritual harlotry, betraying one's trust in the living God. God punished the Canaanites for these sins, and Israel was sent into exile because they engaged mystical powers and consulted mediums, spiritists, and necromancers.

11

Persistent Problem of Ancestral Spirits[54]

One of the greatest problems in the Christian church in many cultures is the persistence of the ancestral cult, from Asia to Africa to Europe and beyond. This is true for both mission-founded churches and African independent churches. For example, the Zionists of South Africa incorporate their ancestors in their beliefs. When sickness occurs, the Zionists believe this is due to a failure to keep the traditional taboos that offend the ancestors. Zionists then consult the witch doctors.

SYNCHRONISTIC SOLUTIONS IN EARLY EUROPEAN CHURCHES

Attempts have been made throughout history to deal with ancestral cults by accommodating these traditions. During the intense persecution of Christians by Roman emperors before AD 313, Christians began to memorialise the martyrs by conducting annual services at the grave to remember their lives. Prayers were offered to God, the martyrs' history was told, and the Eucharist observed.

Gradually, these innocent ways of honouring the dead were corrupted when some church leaders began incorporating traditional European religious beliefs. Added to the martyrs who were memorialized were other *saints*, mainly holy men and women who entered monasteries. By the fifth century, Mary, the mother of Jesus, was included. During the centuries following Constantine, this process of syncretizing European traditional religion with Christianity became even more formalized.

> Just as the pagans had once prayed to certain gods and goddesses for help, so now these new Christians began to visit the graves of Christian martyrs, to prize relics of their life (a bit of robe, bones etc.), much as they had once prized fetishes to ward off evil, and to pray to them as friends in heaven whose intercession before God was very effective. The veneration for saints, about who (and their relics) many miracle stories are told, seems to have filled the vacuum left by the disappearance of the pagan gods who had been very popular with the common folk. They became personal protectors, and the guardians of towns, trades, or peoples in special need, just as the old gods had been. Further, just as pagans had been accustomed to implore the aid of certain mother goddesses, such as Demeter (the earth mother), Isis, Ishtar, or Cybele, so now the Virgin Mary, *the mother of God*, began to have a large place in the devotional life of the Christians both East and West.[55]

"The veneration of saints, beginning with the cult of martyrs, has been a hallmark of the Catholic Church."[56] Today, the Roman Catholic Church explains these practices through the concepts of the *mystical body of Christ* and the *Communion of the Saints,*[57] basing their beliefs on implications from 1 Corinthians 12:12-31, Ephesians 1:22-23, and other verses.

SUGGESTIONS BY SOME LEADERS IN AFRICA

Similarly, some leaders in Africa are accommodating to the ancestral cult. Charles Nyamiti, professor in the Catholic University of Eastern Africa in Nairobi, Kenya, affirms:

> Since ancestral veneration is one of the central items of African Traditional Religion, it would be in keeping with the African traditional religiosity to transform and Christianise this cult and to make it, in a certain sense, one of the central elements of the life in the African churches.[58]

Some Zulu Roman Catholics in South Africa participate in a Christian burial, but they also participate in a ceremony six months later in which the ancestors are invited to "come back home" to protect them and no contradiction is seen in this. "They are conscious of the worth and the goodness of the ancestor cult, and they see nothing basically wrong with it."[59] This has strengthened the Christians' link with their ancestors by baptizing ATR and robing traditional beliefs in Christian garb.

Jean-Marc Éla asks the question: "Can we be at peace with our conscience, if conversion requires that we live separated from the dead of our family, without any possibility of contact with them in the periods of crisis?" He further enquires: "Is there any place in our life in Jesus Christ for maintaining a relationship between the living and the dead? Or must Africans break their relationships with their ancestors if they are to be converted to the gospel?"[60]

Some mainline Protestant church leaders have proposed accommodation to the ancestral cult by incorporating the African ancestors in the Communion of Saints. Over fifty years ago John Taylor, the British Anglican, wrote: "Is it not time for the church to learn to give the Communion of Saints the centrality which the soul of Africa craves?" He continued:

> To ask for the prayers of others in this life, and to know that they rely on mine, does not show any lack of faith in the all-sufficiency of God. Then, in the same faith, let me ask for their prayers still, and offer mine for them, even when death has divided us. They pray for me, I may believe, with clearer understanding, but I for them in ignorance, though still in love.[61]

Today, many of Africa's theologians are following this suggestion of John Taylor in developing the doctrine of Communion of Saints with an emphasis on universalism. Edward Fasholé-Luke fears that all will be lost "unless the churches develop a theology of the Communion of Saints that will satisfy the passionate desire of Africans, Christian and non-Christian alike, to be linked with their dead ancestors."[62] He believes it is through the Eucharist that "we can and do live with our dead in a way which is profoundly true to man's nature." It is during the time of the Eucharist that "African Christians can pray for their ancestors and plead that the one, all-sufficient sacrifice of Christ may be effective in their case also."[63] *All the ancestors* are in the great body of Saints, according to Fasholé-Luke.

AN EVANGELICAL RESPONSE

Although prayers to and for the departed dead are taught by some church leaders, this practice is based on tradition, not Scripture. The biblical prohibition of divination and communicating with the dead eliminate any compatibility of the cult of ancestors with Christianity.

Contrary to what Father Nxumalo found when interviewing Zulu Christians, we have found a uniform rejection of the ancestral cult among the members of the Africa Inland Church in Kenya, as well as independent churches which broke away from the Africa Inland Church.

There are formidable reasons for believing that these so-called *ancestral spirits* are not truly the African ancestors but unclean spirits. Apart from biblical teaching, we found in our research that Kenyan Christians believe that the living-dead are evil, acting contrary to Christ. All Christians whom we interviewed, without exception, rejected the ancestral cult as *incompatible with Christ.*

The conduct and attitude of these *ancestral spirits* towards their *family members* is cruel, harsh, selfish, unkind, hostile, and unforgiving. They are so demanding and cruel that we cannot imagine them to be true ancestors of the people. These *ancestral spirits* claim to do more than any human being can do, such as causing a barren woman to bear children, healing the sick, sending rain, or predicting the future. Can a human being do these things? Bishop Rev. Charles Salalah researched his own people, the Basukuma of Tanzania, and concluded:

> This study holds the view that the ancestral cult among the Basukuma and perhaps other African peoples too, is a manifestation of the devils' and demons' activities of leading people away from worshipping the true God. Demons may rightly be called *angels* of the devil, who deceive people into the belief that man is capable of communicating with the dead, and that the dead are able to harm the living.

TOWARDS A BIBLICAL SOLUTION

There is a great need in Africa for Christian believers to remember their departed ancestors. Memorializing the dead has precedent in the Scriptures and is surely sanctioned by the Bible. Whether this is through the naming of children after their forefathers, erecting monuments, or through dedicating furniture in churches in the memory of dead loved ones, the Christian church needs to assist believers in finding ways to honour and remember their departed loved ones in satisfactory ways.

Apart from creative and indigenous efforts to keep the memory of dead believers alive, we believe that any solution must include the following truths found in this one phrase: *Faith in the living God within the community of believers according to the Scriptures.* Following are some broad guidelines for the basis of an evangelical solution to the problem of ancestral spirits.

The Living God

Christians need to know who God is according to the Scriptures. Solid, biblical teaching on the Being, attributes, and works of God must be instilled within the hearts of all believers.

When professing Christians resort to the ancestral spirits or traditional help in time of trouble, they reflect a failure to trust God and give him his rightful place of supremacy. Jesus Christ is all that we need. He is our Saviour, our Lord and Master, our Shepherd and Provider, and our Keeper and Guide. The riches of Scripture concerning the work of the Father, Son, and Holy Spirit in and for believers must be imparted to *all* believers.

Faith

There are two kinds of faith: *mental assent* to the Christian creed and *personal trust* in the living God. While the first kind of faith is important, it has no saving value. Even demons believe (James 2:19)! Many people profess to be Christian. They are baptised members of the church, attend church services, and may even take leadership roles, but they do not *know* God through *trusting in Jesus Christ*. They have never repented of their sins and personally trusted in Christ alone to forgive their sins.

Consequently, when these individuals face problems in life, they readily fall away from their mental assent to Christian faith and resort to traditional help from the ancestors. The phenomenal growth of the Christian church in Africa does not necessarily reflect the true number of the converted.

Within the Community of Believers

When seeking to deal with the problem of the ancestral cult among the true believers in Christ, the vital, functioning role of the body of Christ is essential. This includes fellowship of believers with prayer, the study of God's Word with application to life, and words of encouragement. When anyone becomes sick or falls into a time of trouble, fellow Christians should visit with them for encouragement from the Word and with prayer.

Where there is a living faith in Jesus Christ and where the community of believers is functioning as they should, there will be great deliverance from the temptations of traditional religion.

According to the Scripture

Scripture is the means by which we obtain personal faith in the living God and grow in our faith and obedience. Faith comes by hearing and reading the Word of God (Romans 10:17). God breathes out his Spirit and grants his people faith as they prayerfully meditate upon the Word of God. Only as the Christian church returns to the Scripture and submits to its judgement, only as she continues to be judged and reformed by the Scriptures, can Christianity be God's answer to mankind's problems.

Traditional African belief in the ancestral spirits is one of those items in ATR that is totally incompatible with the Christian faith. Apart from memorializing the dead as mentioned above, there must be deliverance from traditional captivity through the blood of Christ. Rev Daidanso of Chad referred to Jesus's words to Peter, "Feed my sheep" (John 21:15, 17). Daidanso contends that if the traditional African comes to Christ, he needs to be delivered. Jesus's words to the African pastor are: *Deliver my sheep.*

In Chad, a new believer is asked if he or she has any object which has been associated with the spirits. If so, they bring all those objects out and they are burned while the Christians sing. This is a testimony of the new believer that requires courage. This act of burning those objects is a clear sign of one's commitment to Jesus Christ for salvation and deliverance. If the new believer refuses to burn the fetishes, this reveals fear in him or her. Many people are saved out of ATR but remain bound to the occult. They need to be delivered by claiming the blood of Christ.

In addition to deliverance according to the Scripture, however, believers must also be taught. "*Feed my sheep.*" Christians in Africa need clear teachings from Scripture. Daidanso says that because people are not instructed in the ways of God, these immature Christians return to the spirits during times of sickness and death. ATR becomes a real problem to the African church when suffering comes. Sickness and death lead the people back to ATR. *Thus, the African pastor must both deliver and feed the sheep.*[64]

DEMONIZATION IN BIBLICAL PERSPECTIVE

The topic of demonization has divided the Christian community around the world. Can a believer be demon possessed?

Demonization and Demon Possession

The Bible speaks of demons *inhabiting* a human being. The Greek word for *demon possession* occurs twelve times in the Gospels and means simply "to be possessed by a demon." In 1977 Merrill Unger defined *demon possession* as "a condition in which one or more evil spirits or demons inhabit the body of a human being and can *take complete control* of their victim at will" (emphasis mine). Since a Christian is indwelled by the Holy Spirit, Unger at that time concluded that an evil spirit could not dwell within a Christian.[65]

But after further study and reflection Unger altered his opinion. He lamented that *demon possession* has been applied to all cases of demon oppression. He concluded that *demon possession* should be reserved for "the basest and most enslaving forms [of demonization], such as those represented by the demoniac of Gadara."[66] Instead of using the term *demon possession*, Unger prefers *demonization* or *demonized*, referring to someone under the influence of an evil spirit but not possessed by the spirit.

Timothy Warner suggests degrees of demonization.[67] First degree is *oppression* when the demon is outside a person but oppresses the person, leading the person to sin. Second degree is *obsession* when the demon succeeds in affecting a function of the person such as the mind or emotions. The third degree is *inhabitation* when the demon physically enters the person and gains a foothold within and takes possession of the person.

We conclude that whenever a person is born of the Spirit, that person is indwelled by the Holy Spirit who marks the born-again Christian as a child of God. In this light, no Christian can be demon possessed. But whenever Christians neglect the spiritual disciplines of faithful prayer and meditation on Scripture, and live in disobedience to God, they can be demonized, meaning the evil spirits may oppress and torment a believer.

Christian Help for those Demonized and Demon Possessed

Sadly, there is no basis for believing that demonization is no longer a problem today. The problem is found in America, Africa, Asia, and elsewhere. During his 38 years of ministry as a medical missionary in China during the 19th century, Dr John Nevius chronicled the similarities of demon possession in the Gospels and what he found in China. He also recorded the many testimonies of successful exorcism of those spirits.[68] Nevertheless, great care must be taken not to become unbalanced.

Discernment Is Required

The symptoms of mental disorders or chemical imbalances are real and very similar to demonization. Despite the many years of experience in exorcism, Dr Kurt Koch has never felt able to tell a person they were demon possessed. *We must beware of the tendency of many to blame everything on demons.*

Count on Divine Protection

Care should be taken not to approach demonization with a cavalier attitude. A believer must be rightly related to the Lord with sins confessed and trusting in the power of the blood of Jesus. Nevertheless, a Christian need not fear. Christ assured his disciples that "*Nothing will harm you*" when dealing with the evil spirits (Luke 10:19, NIV, emphasis mine).

Deliverance through the Power of Christ

Deliverance is always and only possible through the name of Jesus Christ. Commanding the spirits in Jesus's name has great power when spoken by one who is cleansed by the blood of Christ. However, this formula is not magical.

Exorcism depends on Christ and his shed blood, not on the formula, "in the name of Jesus."

Perseverance Unto Victory

Even Jesus's disciples found resistance to their efforts to cast out spirits (Mark 9:14-29). Extraordinary, united prayer with other believers with fasting may be required. One person may be too weak, and exorcism of spirits may require the united efforts of several believers.

Break Ties with Occult Objects and Relationships

Most importantly, evil spirits develop special relationships with objects associated with them. This requires a believer to burn and destroy all occult objects in their possession. They also may need to break off relationships with former friends who engage in the world of the occult.

CONCLUSION

We conclude that *the activity of evil spirits is real* and is witnessed both by Scripture and the experience in African Traditional Religion. But we also affirm that *the power of the gospel of Jesus Christ can overcome darkness.*

It is a known fact that in lands where the gospel is preached and believed, the activities of demons are quieted. For example, the Kamba ancestral spirits were especially troublesome in Mumbuni, Machakos, Kenya, an old place of sacrifice, "but by the 1920s the noticeable spirit activity had completely vanished" after the conversion of the Kamba and the building of the church on that very place of sacrifice.[69]

THE SUPREME BEING

12

Light Found in the Supreme Being of African Traditional Religion

As we commence our study of the *supreme being* in ATR, we find it necessary to emphasise once again the diversity and ambiguity of beliefs across African Traditional Religions. The weakness of this chapter is the false appearance that traditional religious beliefs were systematic, uniform, and marked by clarity. For all the strength that John Mbiti provides in his book, *Concepts of God in Africa* (1970), he infers a fullness of African understanding of God that is not present in each community.

For example, the supreme being *Modimu* of the Sotho in South Africa does not speak, *Mawu Anlo-Ewe* of Ghana is said to be both male and female, and *Mulungu* of the Kamba in Kenya is so mysterious and distant that many scholars consider *Mulungu* to be impersonal. Even Kivuto Ndeti, a Mukamba, states: "*Mulungu* is an extremely impersonal force which is rarely mentioned or called upon for personal gains or triumphs."[70]

Nevertheless, sufficient light of general revelation has broken through to cause the African concept of the supreme being to be a positive bridge for understanding the biblical teaching of the God and Father of our Lord Jesus Christ.

OVERLAP OF CHARACTERISTICS BETWEEN GOD AND THE SUPREME BEING

No African community lacks a name for the supreme being. All followers of ATR believe in and accept the reality of a supreme being who created the universe.

The following characteristics of God the Father correspond to characteristics of the supreme being in which many African communities traditionally believe.

- **God is Spirit.** God has no body. He is invisible. He is likened to wind which cannot be seen but is known by its effects. So, too, is the understanding of the supreme being. Of interest is that no material idol has been found in Africa, except in West Africa where *Mawu* is represented by a wooden statue.[71]
- **God is unique.** God is unlike anything or anyone we may know. Uniquely, he has no limitations. Similarly, the Ruanda say: "There is none to equal *Imana*."
- **God is transcendent (highly exalted, distant).** God is highly exalted, the *one High-Up*, beyond human comprehension and mysterious. Across the continent, Africans believe this characteristic is true of the supreme being.
- **God is everlasting.** Another attribute which sets God apart is that he has no beginning. Whatever one may say about traditional belief in ancestral spirits, nature spirits, and divinities, they were all created. God was not. He is *The Everlasting One*, *The One who remains and does not die.*
- **God is personal.** God is personal. There has been much scholarly debate over whether the supreme being in ATR is personal or impersonal – a person or an *it*. Some peoples have greater clarity than others. But we have concluded that the supreme being in Africa is generally a personal being, not an impersonal *it*, although ambiguity often prevails.
- **God knows all things.** God the Father knows all things. Some scholars object to the suggestion that the supreme being in Africa knows all things, saying that omniscience is a Greek idea. These scholars do not recognise that the omniscience of God is found in biblical revelation in the Hebrew Old Testament (e.g., Psalm 139) long before the introduction of Greek thought. Regardless, we have no evidence that the supreme being in Africa has limited understanding.
- **God is present everywhere.** As Spirit, God is present in all places. The Akan compare the supreme being to the wind, which is invisible, but found everywhere. Omnipresence may be an abstract concept, but in practice traditional Africans do not believe they can go anywhere where the supreme being is not found.

- **God is almighty.** When all other help fails, people turn to God. If prayers are not heard, it is not because of the weakness of God, as nothing is too hard for him. Traditional Africans believe in the almighty power of the supreme being, although some do not believe that the supreme being will act on their behalf.
- **God is kind, merciful, and good.** The former attributes of God and their correspondence to the supreme being in ATR are rather well documented, but the kindness, mercy, and goodness of God are not as prominent. Nevertheless, for two reasons we believe that in some measure Africans believe in a supreme being who is kind, merciful, and good: we find little evidence that traditional Africans blamed God for not being kind and merciful and numerous peoples refer to rain and food as evidence of the goodness of God. We believe the fullness of knowing the love and mercy of God awaited the coming of the gospel, but the gospel did not introduce a surprise or a contradiction to their former understanding.
- **God is holy.** The Triune God is holy. While little is said directly in ATR about holiness, the supreme being is the uncreated creator who is transcendent above the world and is above any fault. We can infer from this that the supreme being in ATR is holy.
- Seldom do the peoples of Africa charge the supreme being with failure or wrongdoing, even when tragedy strikes the family. While the problem of evil confronts the African as much as anywhere else in the world, traditional African people believe that the supreme being is good despite pain and suffering.

WORKS OF GOD THAT CORRELATE WITH THE SUPREME BEING

In addition to some important shared characteristics, the following works of God the Father correspond to the supreme being in which many African communities traditionally believe.

- **God created the world.** God is the Creator of all things. Similarly, the belief that the supreme being created all things is the most widely held theological belief in Africa. The various names of the supreme being reflect this belief: *Architect, Molder, Fashioner*, and *Originator*.

In addition, many traditional stories narrate the creative work of the supreme being.

- **God protects and saves.** The book of James tells us that all good things come from God.[72] Similarly, ATR recognises the supreme being's continued involvement in the affairs of the world. The supreme being is the one who provides food, sunshine, rain, children, health, and protection. These are gifts from him.

WORSHIP PRACTICES OF THE SUPREME BEING

The English verb *to worship* is defined by Merriam-Webster as "to honour or show reverence for, as a divine being or supernatural power."[73] By that definition one could question whether most traditional Africans worshipped the supreme being. For many traditional Africans, worship of the supreme being was mingled with sacrifices and offerings rendered to ancestral spirits or divinities. Some African peoples did not offer sacrifices or offerings directly to the supreme being on a regular basis at all.

John Mbiti defines worship rather broadly as "man's act or acts of turning to God."[74] It was at times of calamity that most traditional Africans turned to the supreme being in prayer and sacrifices. This "turning to God," as Mbiti says, was primarily for divine help; it did not explicitly express reverence or honour for the supreme being, though implicitly one might argue such prayers acknowledged his supremacy.

Prayer

Prayers are by far the most common means of "turning to" the supreme being. Most prayers are brief and to the point, beseeching him for some particular need and requests for health, protection, and guidance.

Some Africans prayed daily. Many observed religious rites during the four transitional periods in life, namely birth, initiation, marriage, and death. For agricultural peoples, religious rites were performed at the time of planting and harvesting. Hunters sought help at the time of hunting. Warriors sought aid during the time of war or cattle raiding.

Praying was as natural and spontaneous as breathing air. This is also evidenced in the lives of Christians in Africa who readily and frequently seek God in prayer, far more naturally than most western Christians.

Formal and Informal Worship

Formal worship for the community often took place in a grove of special trees or under a particular kind of tree such as an ancient, durable fig tree. Some peoples did erect mud temples. During formal worship, religious specialists led the ceremonies.

Informal worship was led by the head of the family who gave thanks and petitions at the homestead. Such worship may have been on a regular basis, such as sunrise and sunset, or irregular times during crises. Anyone could pray or offer sacrifices in times of crisis.

But the worship of the supreme being was not always separate and distinct from the veneration given to the living-dead and divinities. Most importantly, the *worship* of the supreme being was utilitarian, seeking the supreme being for the help they might receive, rather than praising the greatness of the supreme being and thanking him for his goodness. ATR worship was *anthropocentric*, meaning man centred.

CONCLUSION

Is the supreme being found in ATR the same being as the God of Christianity? We believe that the living God disclosed eternal truth to all people through general revelation, but because of the Fall when Adam and Eve disobeyed God's direct command, humanity suppressed that knowledge and the eternal truth of God became darkened and distorted. Despite the clouded vision, God has not left himself without a witness. African traditional belief in the supreme being, the *Creator God*, forms a bridge to proclaim the gospel of Jesus Christ, starting at the beginning: "In the beginning God created the heavens and the earth" (Genesis 1:1).

13

The Supreme Being Worldwide

Contrary to the beliefs of naturalists who have speculated that religious beliefs in one God evolved from the simple to the complex, historical evidence demonstrates the truth taught in the Bible. The Creator God has made himself known to all peoples through general revelation of nature and conscience. Everyone understands intuitively the existence of God (Romans 1:19-20).

Andrew Lang had personally lived with and studied the Australian Aborigines. He discovered that they believed in a High God or Supreme Being, not mere spirits or ghosts. He demonstrated that preliterate peoples were monotheists by tradition and not through missionary teaching.

Wilhelm Schmidt was a Roman Catholic priest who gathered evidence which demonstrated a universal belief in God or many gods among the *primitive cultures* worldwide. This belief, he showed, was "a genuine feature of uncontaminated primitive religion." He declared: "Such a concept of Deity, which is almost indistinguishable from that which obtains in the higher monotheisms of Christianity, Islam, or Judaism, is a religious response to the notion of divine Providence more fundamental than any gradual development from plurality and unity."[75]

INDO-ARYANS

Hinduism in India, the third largest world religion, is a complex religion that encompasses great diversity in its beliefs of gods. Today Hinduism embraces 33 million gods. But the oldest and most important collection of hymns found in the *Veda*, Hindu's sacred text, describes the deity in surprising terms. *Varuna* is:

> The Creator and Sustainer of all things, the omniscient Ruler who watches the whole universe with all-seeing, unsleeping eyes, the compassionate Protector and Helper, the Holy One, from whom Law and Right … proceed, who blesses the righteous, sternly punishes the sinner, pardons the penitent, and confers immortality on the faithful dead.[76]

Clearly, the early Indo-Aryans were monotheists originally.

CHINESE

The Chinese people were very religious from ancient times. In the earliest of ancient Chinese writings, we find reference to *Shang Ti*, the supreme being who was always portrayed as the personal, majestic, and glorious being. *Shang Ti* was the supreme ruler and the one who imparted morality. He was the superior emperor, the ancient supreme being.

Through the course of centuries, however, references to *Shang Ti* decreased in usage. *T'ien* was the more impersonal name for *heaven* or *providence* and became predominant in usage. *T'ien* became known among the Chinese as *T'ien Kung*, the Emperor of Pearl, because he lived in a pearl palace. As the highest god, he allocated duties to the various other gods who assisted in administration.

> The Emperor was the supreme god in the universe. All the gods in heaven and in hell were under his command. This included Buddha, Bod-satt, and ancestors. He had a vast bureaucracy with ministries governing various positions, just as the image of the earthly kingdom during the dynasty period.[77]

The Chinese, like the early Indo-Aryans, first believed in a supreme being but as he receded in their experience, other gods and ancestors took his place.

ARABS

Muhammad allegedly crusaded against the polytheism of the Arabs in Mecca where 360 idols were found, representing each day of the year. Prior to

Muhammad, however, the Arabs believed in a supreme being by the name, *Allah*, the creator of all things. They believed in the unity of the supreme being and his omnipotence. But it was believed that *Allah* handed over the administration of the world to other gods and goddesses whom he endued with power. To these gods the people looked for blessings in their lives.[78]

CONCLUSION

There is overwhelming evidence that belief in the Creator God was universal, but this belief became muddied as he receded in their lives and other gods began taking his place. Belief in one God preceded polytheism or animism. Religion did not evolve into monotheism but *devolved* into paganism.

14

The Supreme Being in Biblical Perspective

Years ago, westerners spoke of Africa as *the Dark Continent.* It is important to acknowledge that cultures without the gospel live in darkness, but not total darkness. God's light of general revelation shines through. There is a real danger of *overstating the light* given by general revelation and *understating the darkness* that prevails. What does the Bible say?

LIGHT GIVEN THROUGH NATURAL REVELATION

God is Spirit and hence invisible (1 Timothy 1:17). Yet the invisible God has revealed himself through creation to all peoples. General revelation, given generally to the whole human race, comes in two forms: nature and conscience.

Nature

"The heavens proclaim the glory of God. The skies display his craftsmanship" (Psalm 19:1). The Bible further teaches: "For ever since the world was created, people have seen the earth and sky. Through everything God made, they can clearly see his invisible qualities – his eternal power and divine nature. So they have no excuse for not knowing God" (Romans 1:20).

Two of the *invisible qualities* of God are manifested in nature: God's *eternal power* and his *divine nature.* These are made known as they see the earth and sky and all that God made (Romans 1:20).

Eternal Power of God

God's eternal power is manifested everywhere in nature for all to see. Who can deny the splendour of God's handiwork in in the heavens as they contemplate the universe with the constellations of stars? Who cannot notice the regular rhythms of the earth with the predictable order of day and night, summer, and winter? Who cannot be amazed at the precision of natural laws that regulate everything? Who does not shudder when the earth shakes with devastating earthquakes, or the seas roar with deafening noise in hurricanes, or the winds howl and whirl in frightening tornadoes which wreak havoc and death across the land? People know by intuition that an Intelligent Being with greater power and wisdom than man possesses has created the universe with the earth.

Divine Nature of God

The divine nature of God is revealed in nature (Romans 1:20). This refers to the totality of God's glorious attributes, especially his power, wisdom, and goodness.

During Paul's missionary journey to Lystra, he healed a man who had never walked. Amazed, nearby pagans cried out: "These men [Paul and Barnabas] are gods in human form!" So, they prepared to offer sacrifices in worship of the apostles. These pagans believed Barnabas was Zeus and Paul was Hermes, Greek gods (Acts 14:11-13).

When Paul began preaching the gospel to them, he declared: God has "never left them without evidence of himself and his goodness. For instance, he sends you rain and good crops and gives you food and joyful hearts" (Acts 14:17). The kindness and goodness of God are displayed through the rain and food he graciously provides.

Conscience

The Creator God has also planted within every human being a knowledge of his law in the form of the unwritten law of the conscience (Romans 2:12-16). Unlike the animal kingdom, human beings know intuitively that not every form of conduct is lawful. Might does not make right. Conscience tells everyone that they are not free to do anything they want. In this way God's righteous character is revealed.

Through the law written in their hearts, people have a sense of right and wrong. Even though sin has corrupted the conscience, by God's grace, sinful humans still have a conscience. When Abraham moved to dwell near the Philistines, he thought: "There is surely no fear of God in this place," so he lied to the king and said Sarah was his sister, not his wife (Genesis 20:11, NIV).

But in fact, the king was more righteous than Abraham for he acted with "a clear conscience and clean hands" (20:5, NIV). The Bible teaches:

> Even Gentiles [pagan nations], who do not have God's written law, show that they know this law when they instinctively obey it, even without having heard it. They demonstrate that God's law is written in their hearts, for their own conscience and thoughts either accuse them or tell them they are doing right (Romans 2:14-15).

Conclusion

According to Scripture, the result of God's general revelation is that "they have no excuse for not knowing God" (Romans 1:20). "For the truth about God is known to them instinctively. God has put this knowledge in their hearts" (1:19, TLB). From nature and conscience human beings know intuitively that God created the world and has laid down laws of conduct.

LIGHT SEEN IN AFRICAN TRADITION

Yusufu Turaki cautions that we must not equate African beliefs about the supreme being with biblical meanings of God. Turaki is rightly concerned that we not read too much into traditional African beliefs. We must study ATR inductively and understand African beliefs in the way in which Africans understood them.[79]

On the other hand, we must not be afraid to admit that Africans were given more light than western prejudices might allow. Africans, no less than Asians or westerners, are God's image bearers. They are all equally recipients of God's love and common grace. Though most Africans lived without any knowledge of the gospel of Jesus Christ for centuries, they did receive general revelation through nature and conscience. Let us consider the various kinds of general revelation shown to African peoples.

Names for the Supreme Being – Concepts of God[80]

Across Africa, affirmations of God as evidenced in the names of the supreme being number in the thousands. They provide a powerful witness to the general revelation of God to African peoples, but we should never infer from this that the fullness of truth was grasped by all African peoples in the same measure; nor should we read into the names a rich biblical understanding that we derive from Scripture. Some of these names are:

- **Supreme Being:** Great Chief, Sovereign Ruler of the Universe, The Greatest of the Great, Supreme, The Owner of the Sky.
- **Creator:** God the Creator of All Things, The King that Creates, The Very Source of Being, Carver, Architect, The Arch Moulder.
- **Provider and Sustainer:** Giver of Sun and Light, Giver of Rain, Lord Who Upholds the World, The Source of Being Who Sustains the Universe.
- **Judge:** God the Silent but Active Judge.
- **Eternal:** The One Who Remains and Does Not Die, The Everlasting One, He Who Is There Now as from Ancient Times, The Eternal One.
- **Spirit**: Great Spirit, The King Invisible.
- **Transcendent and Great:** King Who Lives in the Sky and His Clothes Touch and Roll on the Ground, King of Heaven, God Above.
- **Omnipresent** (present everywhere): He Who Is Everywhere.
- **Omnipotent** (all powerful): The Impregnable, Almighty, He Who Alone Can Speak and Accomplish His Words.
- **Omniscient** (knows all things): He Who Sees All, He Who Hears and Sees Everything, The Discerner of the Hearts, The Wise One.
- **Self-Existent** (existing of oneself independently of any other being or cause): He Who Is of Himself, The First, Who Has Always Been in Existence, and Would Never Die.
- **Faithful:** The Dependable.
- **Kind and Merciful:** Consoler, Comforter Who Gives Salvation, God the Benefactor, The Merciful God.
- **Holy:** The Pure King.
- **Approachable:** He in Whom You Confide Troubles Which Come upon You.
- **Mysterious:** The Unknown, One Known but Never Fully Known, The Unexplainable.
- **Ancestor:** Great Ancestor, Grandfather, Grandmother.

Many of the African name statements about the supreme being are startling in their splendour. Among the Zulu, a very powerful and warlike nation, the supreme being is described as "He who roars so that all the nations are struck with fear," Among the Yoruba he is known as "He who sees both the inside and outside (of man)." The Gikuyu say that the supreme being is "all alone, without father or mother and without companions." The Akan respond when asked, "How are you?" with the words, "By God's grace, I am well." The Pygmies of Central Africa speak of him poetically:

> In the beginning was God.
> Today is God,
> Tomorrow will be God.
> Who can make an image of God?
> He has no body.
> He is a word which comes out of your mouth.
> That word! It is no more,
> It is past, and still it lives!
> So is God.[81]

Knowledge of Human Nature

Not only do traditional Africans possess knowledge about God and something of his attributes through their understanding of the supreme being, but many ATR beliefs also demonstrate some understanding of the nature of humans.

The Spiritual Nature of Human Beings

Nowhere across Africa do traditional peoples think men and women were composed only of matter. Human beings have a spiritual component in addition to the physical. Humanity has both a body and soul. Communities speak of this spiritual nature in different ways, such as: *heart*, *head*, *mind*, *soul*, or *breath*.

Life after Death

The materialistic, naturalistic view of human beings so common among westerners today was totally foreign to Africans in the past. In ATR, though the physical body falls ill and dies, the spirit continues to live on in a life much like the one known in real life today.

Original State of Human Beings

Some African communities have various beliefs of an original state of happiness, childlike innocence, and immortality, although these traditions are not found among most Africans.

A few African communities have traditions that the supreme being was in close fellowship with man at one time. As these few African peoples look back into the golden age of the past, they remember a time when they lived close to the supreme being. During that time death was unknown. Men and women lived without dying. They had all the provisions needed and lived in happiness. Some people say that the supreme being visited them frequently and even lived among them. It was like a family relationship.

Some, like the Ashanti and Akan, pictured the supreme being living in the nearby heavens, close enough for people to touch him. When an old woman began pounding her grain with her long pestle, she accidentally jabbed the supreme being. Every time she did so, he moved further away up into heaven.

The Mende say that the supreme being broke his fellowship with man because people asked him too many questions. Others say that he withdrew because the smoke from grass fires irritated his eyes.

According to the Bambuti, Banyarwanda, Barotse, Bushman, Chagga, and Elgeyo, the supreme being gave to man a particular law to obey. When man broke that law, the supreme being separated from them.

The Yoruba believed that in the beginning heaven was closer to earth and people could travel to heaven as they wished and have direct contact with the supreme being. During this golden age, there were no limitations to communication between heaven and earth. Some traditions say that this all changed when a woman with a dirty hand touched the unsoiled face of heaven, and other traditions say that a greedy person took too much food from heaven. Whatever the cause, separation from the supreme being took place when a human being offended him.

Evidence of Common Grace in Africa

Many other indications show that Africa was endowed with common grace:

- Africans recognised that the supreme being deserved honour and worship. Blood sacrifices and offerings of first fruits are a means of placating and honouring the supreme being.

- Retribution and punishment occur when someone disobeys traditions. Sacrifices are necessary to restore harmony.
- Whenever a need arises, people can turn to the supreme being in prayer.
- The prominent belief of the supernatural in ATR has contributed to African receptivity to the gospel.

Generally, Bible translators have adopted the African names for God when translating Scripture into various African languages. Although certain problems have arisen, Christian translators believed there was sufficient similarity between the concept of the supreme being and God (*Yahweh*) that the Christian church could purge away any error and give a biblical meaning to the African names for God.

Preparation for the Gospel in ATR

The measure of light found in African Traditional Religion, even if limited or distorted, has served as a royal road by which the gospel can be communicated to people steeped in ATR. African hearts have been prepared for Christ through God's common grace.

Many of the beliefs of traditional Africans are compatible with the teachings of Scripture. Could it be that communication of the Christian faith to Africans is better understood than by the Hindu or the Buddhist *because* of ATR? Beliefs in the Creator God, the supernatural, a knowledge of right and wrong, punishment for wrongdoing, blood sacrifices to appease anger, the spiritual nature of human beings with life after death, and belief in spirits are all compatible with Christianity.

This measure of light granted to Africa through God's common grace given to all peoples, has proved to be a bridge for the preaching of the Good News of salvation through Jesus Christ.

Conclusion

Biblically speaking, God never abandoned Africa. He continues to manifest his common grace. ATR prepared Africans for the gospel.

15

Darkness Blinds the Heart According to the Scriptures

We have previously pointed out the errors of mystical powers, divinities, and the relationships with the dead, but what of African people's traditional belief in the supreme being? Isn't this belief the strength of ATR? Indeed, it is; but we believe that, from a biblical perspective, *it is also the most serious error*. Let's explore this further.

MAJOR SINS OF HUMAN BEINGS

A key passage in Romans 1:18–3:20 enumerates dozens of sins which men and women commit against God. But we believe the two major sins which underlie all other sins are these: removing the Creator God from the centre of life and replacing him with pseudo gods.

Removing God

The anger of God is poured out on humanity because people *suppress the truth* revealed in nature and conscience. "But God shows his anger from heaven against all sinful, wicked people who *suppress the truth by their wickedness*" (Romans 1:18, emphasis mine). To *suppress* the truth is to hold it down or to push it away. It is both a conscious and an unconscious act of removing God from the centre of life.

Truth in the New Testament is not simply a proposition to which we give mental assent. *Truth* is something to be done, to be obeyed. Because God has revealed himself as the Creator of all things, the Ruler over all chiefs, kings, and presidents, he deserves worship and obedience consistent with his status.

This *suppression* is not a one-time event, but an ongoing rebellion, a day-by-day resistance to God's will. Human beings by nature are continually pushing God and his truth away from their lives.

Suppressing the truth or *pushing the truth away* is done when God's revelation is ignored and people choose to live a wicked, unrighteous lifestyle. By living contrary to the revealed will of God, they blot out their knowledge of the truth through persistent disregard for the truth and pursuit of degraded behaviour.

We have seen this suppression evidenced in other world religions. As we have noted previously, literary records of Asians, Arabs, and Europeans all reveal a belief in the Creator God in antiquity. Even during Israel's history under the Old Covenant, and the Christian church under the New Covenant, God's people have persistently moved away from their knowledge of one true God in their worship. Only by God's grace poured out repeatedly in revivals and great awakenings have they returned to true worship of God.

A word of clarification is needed. The Bible teaches that people who have natural revelation *know* God, saying: "yes, they knew God, but they wouldn't worship him as God or even give him thanks" (Romans 1:21). According to Scripture *everyone knows God* in one sense, but they *don't know God* in another sense. General revelation enables everyone to have a limited *intellectual knowledge* of God. They know *about* God. As Phillips translates the verse: "*They knew all the time that there is a God*" (emphasis mine). They know he exists, and they know certain characteristics of God including his commandments.

But they do not know God personally as their Lord and Saviour. The background for the Hebrew word translated by the Greek word *ginosko* in the New Testament, has a deeper meaning than mere intellectual awareness. It involves a personal, intimate knowledge. The word *ginosko* can even refer to sexual intercourse as in Genesis 4:1, "Now Adam *knew* Eve his wife, and she conceived and bore Cain" (ESV, emphasis mine).

The Bible emphatically teaches that the Gentiles do *not* know God in this personal sense (Romans 3:9-20). The scandal is that humanity, apart from the saving knowledge of Jesus Christ, does not honour him as God with acceptable worship and genuine praise from a redeemed heart. They do not keep his commandments. To *know God* is more than intellectual awareness, but an intimate, personal knowledge that leads to genuine repentance, faith, worship, and heartfelt obedience.

Replacing God

As a result of rejecting God, removing God from the centre of their lives, people's hearts and minds became darkened. Listen to the blistering condemnation of men and women who have pushed God away from themselves. Because they would not worship God as he deserved, or give him thanks:

> They began to think up *foolish ideas* of what God was like. As a result, their *minds became dark and confused.* Claiming to be wise, *they instead became utter fools.* And instead of worshipping the glorious, ever-living God, they worshipped idols made to look like mere people and birds and animals and reptiles" (Romans 1:21b-23, emphasis mine).

The more literal rendering of the Greek says: "and *exchanged* the glory of the immortal God for images resembling mortal man and birds and animals and creeping things" (Romans 1:23, ESV, c.f. 1:25, emphasis mine). The English word, *exchanged,* expresses a cultural practice common in Africa. It refers to a bartering, a practice often seen in marketplaces. I give you something I don't want *in exchange* for something you have which I want.

What human beings do not want is "the knowledge of God," as the NIV translates verse 28: "they did not think it worth while to retain the knowledge of God". Shocking! Human beings were given the precious knowledge of the Creator God and his will. Not wanting this truth, sinful man bartered it away in exchange for gods of their own making.

In brief, instead of serving and worshipping the Creator God as revealed to them in nature and conscience, their foolish, darkened hearts create gods of their own choosing. Idolatry is the damning sin of all humans; instead of worshipping the true God, they worship gods of their own making.

In the Old Testament the most prevalent form of idolatry was the worship of images or idols that were made to represent some god. The Hebrew prophets heaped ridicule on these idols by referring to them with demeaning Hebrew words such as: filth, dung, refuse, shameful thing, wicked, false, nothingness as a breath of air (c.f. Isaiah 44:9-20).

Africans may feel exempt of this charge of idolatry by the simple fact that only one image/idol has been found in Africa. By this standard the peoples of

Africa were never idolatrous. In the mid-20th century, we used to sing in western churches a missions song entitled, "From Greenland's Icy Mountains."[82] The second verse included the phrase: "In vain with lavish kindness the gifts of God are strown; the *heathen in his blindness bows down to wood and stone*" (emphasis mine).

However, the New Testament, building on the Old Testament teaching of idolatry, adds a new dimension. Idolatry is "used figuratively of undue obsession with any object less than God."[83] "The idol is whatever claims that loyalty which belongs to God alone."[84] "In a general sense idolatry is the paying of divine honours to any created thing; the ascription of divine power to natural agencies."[85] "In the New Testament, idolatry came to mean not only the giving to any creature or human creation the honour or devotion which belongs to God alone, but the giving to any human desire a precedence over God's will."[86]

Hence, we read that *riches* can be idolatrous whenever someone gives primary affection and devotion to them (Matthew 6:24). *Covetousness* is idolatry because a covetous person is seeking that which God has not given to him; he prefers his own will to the will of God (Ephesians 5:5). *Gluttony* is idolatry because gluttony is an obsession for self-centred desires to indulge in excessive eating contrary to the will of God (Philippians 3:19). *Participating in heathen feasts* amounts to idolatry (1 Corinthians 10:14-22). *Pride* is the most heinous form of idolatry. A self-centred person who chooses his way over God's way commits idolatry. Humans, by choosing their own will over God's will, make themselves into their own little gods.

CONCLUSION

From this biblical study, we see that the heart of idolatry is the removing of God from his rightful position as Lord and replacing him with gods of human design. For the *creature* to treasure any desire, person, or object more than the *Creator* and his perfect will is to commit idolatry.

16

Darkness in African Traditional Religion

Africans are one with the whole human race in pushing God away from the centre of life and replacing him with gods of their own making, their chief god being self with pride, envy, covetousness, and lust of the flesh. But that is not the question being addressed here.

The question is: does African Traditional Religion itself promote and foster idolatry? We believe that ethnographic reports support the biblical teaching that idolatry has pervaded African traditional culture: God has been removed from the centre of life and replaced by other gods.

GOD HAS BEEN REMOVED FROM THE CENTRE OF LIFE

Ethnographic evidence in Africa confirms the teaching of Scripture. Let's look at some examples.

Gikuyu of Kenya

Jomo Kenyatta observed that the Gikuyu called upon the supreme being during the times of crises: at birth, initiation, marriage, and death.

However, *Ngai*, is "a Distant Being and takes but little interest in individuals in their daily walks of life."[87] The affairs of individuals do not concern God, only those of the community. "God lives in the heavens and does not bother with the work or affairs of one man alone. He looks after the whole people or homestead group. There is no one man's religion or sacrifice."[88] Kenyatta then wrote:

> So far as people and things go well and prosper, it is taken for granted that God is pleased in the general behaviour of

> the people and the welfare of the country. In this happy state there is no need for prayers. Indeed it is inadvisable, for *Ngai* must not needlessly be bothered. It is only when humans are in real need that they must approach him, without fear of disturbing him and incurring his wrath.[89]

The significance of this statement is twofold: it is written by a Gikuyu himself and written in the 1930s. Such an explanation of traditional belief might easily be dismissed if uttered by a non-African, but Kenyatta spoke of what he knew personally. Moreover, he spoke of what he knew in the early part of the last century. Many changes have transpired in ATR in the past 100 years, but what Kenyatta affirmed represents belief as he understood it before missionary and European influence was felt.

Turkana of Kenya

The Turkana have not been studied nearly as much as the Gikuyu and Kamba. But it is known that they believe in a supreme being called *Akuj*, the same word for *sky*. He is a person who owns a large homestead with many cattle grazing on evergreen pastures.

Yet P. H. Gulliver reports that *Akuj* is only *potentially* supreme "because, although omnipotence is attributed to him, yet in practice only certain powers are expected of him."[90] The Turkana people *say Akuj* is all-powerful, but no one expects him to work any miracles. He has great power if only one can induce him to work on man's behalf. In practice they do not depend on him for much. If *Akuj* answers prayer, no one gives him thanks or shows him honour. Likewise, if he does not answer prayer, this is also taken as a matter of fact. One can go for weeks, it is reported, without hearing the name of *Akuj*.

The Wazigua of Tanzania

The Wazigua believe that the supreme being was an "awful, unapproachable Power, contact with whom must be maintained through a medium. Like the Pare, they chose the spirits of their ancestors to act as mediators and like the Pare they chose the spirits only of elder males as efficient to act."[91]

The Chagga of Tanzania

Speaking of *Ruwa*, the god of the Chagga, we read: "The truth is that *Ruwa* has long ago ceased to mingle with and care for his creatures, and they on their side seek succour from him only in extreme distress, sacrificing to him at rare intervals just such animals as he has provided them for the purpose."[92]

The Sukuma of Tanzania

According to social anthropologist Hans Cory, what is said of *Likuube,* god of the Sukuma, can also be said of *Mulungu*, god of many East African Bantu. "He is a very remote supreme being, who created the world. *Likuube* is so remote and exalted that he cannot be expected to interfere with the fate of an individual. No sacrifices and prayers can reach him; he has done his work but he is not working anymore because all that is, has never changed."[93]

Though the Sukuma mention *Likuube* in their prayers, it is only by way of introduction, while the prayer itself is directed to the spirits nearer to men. The same kind of sentiment is expressed by the Swazi of Swaziland.

The Mende of Sierra Leone and the Leza of Zimbabwe

Professor Geoffrey Parrinder, who has a helpful discussion on this topic, refers to various peoples. The Mende of Sierra Leone believe that the supreme being retired in the heaven after creation and is little concerned with the activities on earth. He can be approached in times of distress, but normally people use the intermediaries, the divinities, and the ancestors.

The Leza of Zimbabwe have no ceremonies for the supreme being, who is considered too far away and fearful, though they may approach him directly in times of great need. Normally, they pray to the lesser divinities who serve as intermediaries. Parrinder concludes by saying: "In many parts of Africa one finds the strange phenomenon that God is believed in, yet is thought of as so great and remote that he is offered no regular worship."[94]

Dinka of Sudan

John Taylor focuses on the paradox of African belief and practice, that the supreme being is both far away and near. The Dinka sing a song that underlines this paradox:

Great *Deng* is near, and some say 'far' of Divinity.
The Creator is near, and some say, 'he has not reached us.'
Do you not hear, O Divinity?
The black bull of the rain has been released from the moon's
byre,
Do you not hear, O Divinity?[95]

Nupe of Northern Nigeria

Among the Nupe of Northern Nigeria, "the most common and strongly emphasised comment on the nature of the deity is, '*soko Lokpa.*' God is far away, yet in a different sense, a more mystic sense. He is present always and everywhere."[96] Concluding the chapter Taylor wrote:

> But while everywhere there seems to be an underlying conviction that such a God is, it is accompanied, and usually overwhelmed, by the pragmatic knowledge that such a god has gone away. The African myth does not tell of man driven from Paradise, but of God disappearing from the world. It is men, not God, whose voice calls through the desolate garden, where art thou?[97]

John Mbiti refers to this paradox in African Traditional Religion. Mbiti writes: "For most of their life, many African peoples place God in the transcendental plane, making him seem remote from their daily affairs. But they know that he is immanent."[98]

> It is a paradox that they *know* him, and they do not *know* him. He is not a Stranger to them, and yet they are estranged to him; he knows them, but they do not know him. So God confronts [humanity] as the mysterious and incomprehensible, and as indescribable and beyond human vocabulary. This is part of the essential nature of God.[99]

These words of Mbiti are profound and true. Yet we feel constrained to go beyond them in biblical perspective. The peoples of Africa are in solidarity with humanity. The human nature of Africans is identical to the nature of humanity, because all men and women partake of the nature of Adam, the father of the one human race. According to Scripture, all men and women have been given knowledge about God in nature, but all peoples have rejected him and pushed him away (Romans 1:21-22).

Harry Sawyerr wrestles with the question among West Africans, whether they believe in God. He observes that the Akan are among the few people in West Africa who have built temples for the worship of God and assigned priests to offer regular sacrifices to Him. Instead of worshipping God,

> We meet a whole array of lesser gods and the long line of ancestral spirits to whom prayers are offered and who are, indeed, regarded as the more responsible for the day-to-day factors of life. It is in this context that we have to inquire whether the African does in fact 'believe in God.' We recall the remark made earlier that God is thought to be far removed from the affairs of [humanity]. And yet, [people] do always appeal to Him in times of crisis. How then can we reconcile these two contrary attitudes?[100]

His response is that the African's attitude to God reflects his experience and his relationship with his chiefs. Chiefs or kings traditionally ruled the peoples in Africa and these chiefs or kings were approachable only through intermediaries. "For all practical purposes, the chief is distant from ordinary men. He is addressed only through the intermediary, and in turn, he addresses his petitioners only through the intermediary."[101]

In other words, God is treated as one treats the African chief or king. Normally, God is approached through intermediaries, but in times of crises, anyone can approach God directly and immediately, and he listens to them.

Such an approach is painfully inadequate. Sawyerr wrestles with the evidence. God is indeed removed from the centre of life. While the divinities are worshipped regularly and while the ancestors are the prime factors influencing the lives of the Africans, God is, in fact, not worshipped in the same manner.

Sawyerr finds solace in a sociological understanding of the African peoples. The religious beliefs of Africans, Sawyerr says, are a reflection of the sociological structure of the African communities. This may be good anthropology, but it is bad theology. How should we understand ATR from a biblical perspective? Sawyerr never touched the question even though he was a Canon of St. George's Cathedral, Freetown. But it is a central contention of this book that we cannot truly understand or interpret ATR from God's point of view unless we examine ATR through the spectacles of biblical revelation.

Sawyerr's interpretation, however deficient it may be, only confirms the fact that God has been removed from the centre of life. Even as the chiefs and kings were distant from the peoples, generally beyond personal fellowship or communication apart from a crisis, so God is likewise removed; but whereas Sawyerr finds a sociological explanation for this removal, we find a theological basis.

A study of ATR, like the study of history, is a narrative of God seeking and calling people to himself, but people rejecting his love and grace. Instead, God is only the last resort in time of trouble. As the leader of a hunting expedition said after two weeks of bad luck, "I am tired of asking the shades, let us pray to God."[102] Africa has known *about* God through their beliefs in the supreme being, but they have not known God personally. The presence of God is not practiced among the people traditionally because they have been alienated from God through sin. As Rosemary Guillebaud says of *Imana*, the god among the peoples of Ruanda and Burundi:

> Imana is the great Creator, the First Cause of all good. He does not enter into daily life at all, in a practical sense, and yet is continually in the peoples' thoughts . . . *The name of Imana is constantly in the life of the people, even though they do not worship Him*[103] (emphasis mine).

We believe this is true, both from Scriptures and from a study of world cultures. Africans are in solidarity with humanity. They have traditionally removed God from the centre of their lives. He is neither worshipped nor honoured as God should be. They know *about* God but do not truly know him. Pushing God away is the first step towards idolatry.

IDOLATRY IS FOSTERED IN AFRICAN TRADITIONAL RELIGION

Whether Africans have committed idolatry through their traditional beliefs and practices depends on your perspective. In theory one could argue as some

African scholars do, that Africans know and believe in the Creator God who has all power and wisdom whom they worship alone, but they also give homage to the lesser chiefs (divinities and ancestors) who intercede on their behalf before the Creator Chief.

But theory should line up with practice. If people acknowledge their belief in God, they are not atheists *in theory*. But if they live as though there is no God who is sovereign over their lives, then they are practical atheists, meaning they are atheists *in practice*.

Ethnographic evidence has demonstrated that Africans have pushed God from the centre of their lives through the way in which they interact with the supreme being. Apart from crises or ceremonial occasions, traditional Africans live as though the supreme being, and thereby God, are irrelevant.

From a biblical perspective, all human beings are sinners by nature. They have rebelled against God, transgressed his law, and relegated God to the fringes of their lives. Furthermore, they have substituted gods of their own making to which they offer their allegiance and affection (Romans 1:18–3:20; Ephesians 2:1-3).

We believe that the ethnographical evidence from across the African continent confirms that this is equally true of ATR. In one way or another, apart from divine grace, Africans are idolaters along with all humanity.

Africa is a vast continent with 1,000 ethnic communities. We cannot presume to write of all of Africa in this small book. However, we are convinced that the evidence supports the assertion that in the place of God, most African communities have placed the divinities and ancestors in the centre of their lives. Many people argue with reason that West Africa is polytheistic with its belief in divinities. *In practice* the ancestors of many African communities serve as their gods, even *if not in theory*.

We recognise that not all Africans have done this. Generally, divinities are limited to West Africa and the kingdoms of Uganda. Further, the ancestral cult does not play a significant role among certain African communities, such as the Nilo-Hamitic peoples. However, they are no more exempt from idolatry than westerners.

In our limited space we will consider the Kamba, a Bantu community living in Kenya, who exemplify the underlying problem of idolatry among their people.

In our limited field research among the Kamba, we discovered that many traditional Kamba do believe that they honour God more than the ancestors.

They argue that the living share a respectful relationship with their departed relatives since biological death cannot separate the living from their ancestors. The communication and the *communion* with sacrifices and offerings are said to take place between the living and their living-dead.

In their thinking the traditional Kamba distinguish between *Ngai Mumbi* (God the Creator) and the *ngai* (gods) of the family. *Mulungu* (*Ngai Mumbi*) alone has all power. *Mulungu* alone cannot be deceived, they say. The ultimate explanation for everything, including the *aimu (ancestors),* is the Creator God.

But the facts relating to the *aimu* are more complicated. It is not straightforward. We agree with Kivuto Ndeti that the relationship with the Kamba ancestors is "a very complex phenomenon."[104]

The following facts, we believe, demonstrate that the traditional relationship with the *aimu* is idolatrous in practice, if not in theory.

Ethnographic Evidence

The problem is that *in practice* there is very little to distinguish the *worship* given to *Mulungu* and the honour given to the ancestral spirits (*aimu*).

One word in Kikamba for worship is *kuthemba*, "to offer a sacrifice." *Nthembo* is a sacrifice of any kind, including food, beer, blood, drink, or animal sacrifice. This sacrifice was *never* given to the living but restricted to God and the ancestral spirits.

This sacrifice was traditionally given primarily to the ancestors, with God seldom honoured by offerings. There is no clear distinction made between God and the ancestors with reference to sacrifices at the traditional shrines.

The prayers offered in the home during the pouring of the libation, the intercession at the shrines when sacrifices are offered, the religious rites of passage, the prayers and sacrifices offered under the direction of the medicine man, all intermingle the petitions and honour given to the creator (*Ngai Mwatuangi*) and to the gods (*ngai*) of the home (i.e. *aimu*). The following prayers exemplify this assertion.

- When offering libation in the home: "God the Creator, who created and divided the fingers of people (*Ngai Mwatuangi*), drink this water, and you, my father and grandfather, drink this water."
- "*Kyunda,* drink this wine and give to *Mutyanyungu*; and *Mutyanyungu*, give *Isenge*, and you, *Isenge*, give *Mundo*; and you, God who is the

> shepherd, also drink this wine; and all of you, preserve the family because if you let it be destroyed where will you be coming to visit?"

Prayers for divine assistance are addressed to the ancestral spirits without referring to the Creator God.

- Before going on safari, a Mukamba prays: "Father, grandfather, and my mother's brother and the rest of the family, drink this wine and protect me on the way."
- When praying for milk given by cows, a Mukamba says: "Father and mother, we give milk and then give us more milk for this cow does not have any."

Evidence shows that the Kamba confessed to the ancestors when they failed to give them their due respect. They praised the ancestors during times of abundance; they offered prayers of supplication to the ancestors when sickness or famine occurred.

In other prayers, the Creator God is plainly and unmistakably associated with all the other spirits in equal fashion. They are all treated the same

- "Our ancestors, drink from there with our father, mother, grandmother, our daughters, the one who perished with the bow and arrows, then pass it on to all those who disappeared, and are forgotten, and you, those who died without wives, drink from there, then let the bowl go because it is not yours, God the Divider, *Kathambi*, and *Muviti*, drink or eat our food from here, receive yours, then, *Ngai Mwatuangi*, drink yours together with the others."
- "God (*Ngai Mwatuangi*), we pray to you and to our ancestors, and also to *Kathambi* and *Muviti,* we want you all to . . . for us."

We concur with the conclusion of Bishop Charles Salalah who studied the beliefs and practices of his own people, the Basukuma in Tanzania:

> Although Mbiti and Pritchard claim that African peoples worship or sacrifice to God when they sacrifice to the spirits, the Basukuma practice seems to be too evasive for one to

> come up with an unequivocal [clear] view. There are no shrines devoted to God, neither are there priests set apart for him. He is recognised as the Creator of all things and is not put on the same level with ancestors. However, when it comes to the question of actual worship and sacrificing to him, evidence seems to be inconclusive.[105]

Bishop Salalah questions Mbiti's assumption that the ancestors are always and only intermediaries between God and man.

> The Basukuma monotheistic concept cannot be affirmed without some qualifying statements. God's place in their religion is obscured by ancestral spirits, who are the centre of worship in people's daily lives. Mbiti's contention that ancestors are intermediaries between God and man, and that people worship Him through ancestral spirits, does not appear to be apparent among the Basukuma.[106]

Christian Testimony

The pioneering Protestant missions which entered Kenya by the turn of the 20th century formed a united stand against certain traditional practices such as witchcraft and activities of the ancestors. Christian converts were obligated to abstain from such practices.

It is natural, perhaps, that Christians in mission-founded churches would speak negatively of the traditional relationship with the dead. But critical scholars today believe that authentic *African* Christianity can only be found among African-initiated churches which have broken away from mission-founded churches. Interestingly, while the largest Protestant church among the Kamba is the Africa Inland Church, the churches that broke away from the AIC take a similar stance on African traditions except for one practice: they will baptise polygamous converts with their wives while the AIC has refused to do so. This appears to negate the position of critical scholars.

These African-initiated churches stand shoulder to shoulder with members of the Africa Inland Church in their opposition to traditional relationships with the dead (*aimu*). For example, the Good News Church of Africa forbids her members to participate in the ancestral cult by giving food or drink to the ancestors daily at mealtime, attending sacrificial rites for ancestors, seeking help from the ancestors, appeasing the ancestors through traditional means, or communicating with the ancestors. Their reason? They say it is unbiblical and satanic.[107]

CONCLUSION

The biblical perspective of the human condition is clearly outlined in Romans 1:18–3:20. No exceptions! We may choose to reject biblical teaching, but we cannot change it. To be biblical we must admit that God's judgement on all peoples is that they have pushed God from the centre of their lives and replaced him with gods of their own making. In turn God gave people over to what they wanted: "So God abandoned them to do whatever shameful things their hearts desired" including the worship of created things (Romans 1:24).

Instead of embracing biblical truth, a wide range of theologians in both Africa and in western nations have written books in which they recommend incorporating the African ancestors and divinities into Christian theology.[108]

But according to the Bible, the beliefs of non-Christian religions are not benign beliefs that can be incorporated into Christian theology. The Bible states that the sacrifices offered in non-Christian worship are offered to demons and not to God (1 Corinthians 10:20). God denounces all efforts to speak with the dead because evil spirits *impersonate* the spirits of the dead. The Bible warns of idolatry, so prevalent in all communities around the world. Special honours, supplications, and worship are offered to the creatures instead of the Creator, whether divinities and ancestors in Africa, or the superstars, pursuit of wealth, or lustful desires in the West. No one is exempt from this vile temptation. We conclude by concurring with Adeyemo who wrote:

> In the New Testament, both Jesus Christ and His apostles taught and demonstrated that only God is to be worshipped. Any attempt to worship anyone else besides the triune God is a perversion of truth. This is Satan's avid effort to secure for himself what belongs properly to God alone (Matthew 4:9). Undue deference paid to [people] verges at times on worship and this is resisted by the disciples (Acts 10:25, 26;

14:11-14). Explicit commands are given in the Bible not to worship any other be it . . . or ancestors, except the Living God (Exodus 20:3; Deuteronomy 4:14-20; Job 31:24-28; Colossians 2:18). In the light of this sharp distinction, this writer understands worship in the traditional religion as idolatry with the best commentary in Romans 1:21-25 and 1 Corinthians 8:1-7).[109]

CONCLUDING THOUGHTS

17

Historical Perspectives on Syncretism

The goal of the church of Jesus Christ anywhere in the world is to make Christ incarnate among the peoples. Because the light of general revelation has been granted to all people made in the image of God, every culture can be transformed to conform more to the will of God. Because of the darkness that prevails in the human heart due to sinful nature, every culture is permeated with sinful elements that need to be purged.

Failure to incarnate the gospel within one's own culture will lead to one of two errors: a *foreign church* that is not contextualised, or a *syncretistic church* which compromises the truth of the gospel. The Bible is the standard by which we judge whether a cultural element conforms to God's will or is capable of being transformed. Some cultural elements, according to the Bible, are so unbiblical that they must be abandoned altogether. This problem is not new. As we conclude the study of light and darkness found within African Traditional Religion, we must examine the historic problem of syncretism within the global church.

DESCRIPTION OF SYNCRETISM

The English word, *syncretism*, comes from a Greek word which was derived from a practice of ancient Cretans. The clans on the island of Crete continually fought with each other, but when attacked from outside the clans of Crete joined together to fight the common enemy. In other words, the warring peoples of Crete joined together (*syn-crete*). Syncretism is uniting warring brothers.

Syncretism has been defined as "the union of two or more opposite beliefs, so that the synthesised form is a new thing"[110] and as "the union of two opposite forces, beliefs, systems or tenets so that the united form is a new thing, neither one nor the other."[111]

Cultural adaptation or the absorption of cultural ideas and practices in a local Christian community is not necessarily syncretistic, although it can be. If the cultural ideas and practices are consistent with the Scriptures and do not conflict with the essential message and world view of the Bible, then syncretism is not a problem.

Syncretism grows out of a denial of any unique revelation or exclusive faith. When people do not believe the Bible is the inerrant word of God, meaning that it contains no faults or mistakes, then theology becomes relative and therefore open to incorporating other unbiblical ideas. Syncretism is the attempt to unite, harmonise, or fuse together diverse beliefs of one religion with conflicting beliefs of another. This may occur consciously and deliberately by church leaders and theologians who seek to accommodate culture. This kind of syncretism moves from top to bottom. More often, however, syncretism is spontaneous, moving from bottom up when converts unconsciously bring conflicting elements from their old religion or their culture into their newly adopted religion.

SYNCRETISM IN HISTORY

The problem of syncretism is nothing new. From the earliest times, people have struggled to keep their worship of God pure, and often their efforts to safeguard purity result in something other than faith in and following of the One True God.

One Old Testament example tells of a time when foreigners came to live in Israel, "and though they [the new residents] worshiped the Lord, they continued to follow their own gods according to the religious customs of the nations from which they came" (2 Kings 17:33).

By the time of Jesus, some Jewish religious leaders had instituted more than 600 additional rules in their efforts to obey God's decrees. Jesus told them, "'[you] teach man-made ideas as commands from God.' For you ignore God's law and substitute your own tradition" (Mark 7:7-8).

The apostle Paul's letters seem to indicate the early church was also tempted with syncretism, but with Jesus's recent example and the apostle's teachings, early Christians predominantly remained faithful to the faith handed down to them.

Fourth Century through the Renaissance Period

A tidal wave of syncretism began when Constantine, emperor of the Roman Empire, was converted to Christianity in AD 312, and the empire eventually made Christianity the official religion in AD 381. Large numbers of people became Christians throughout this period, but they remained largely uneducated in Christian theology. These first-generation Christians combined old pagan beliefs and practices with the teachings of the Bible much like the Old Testament example of foreigners when they came to live in Israel. By AD 500 most of the population of the Roman Empire professed to be Christian, but many people were Christian in name only and were mostly biblically untaught.

"The pagan custom of raising [humans] to the rank of gods or demigods against which the Christian apologists so vigorously protested crept into the church in the honours paid to the apostles, martyrs, and angels."[112] It has been reported that some Christian leaders rejoiced in the fact that martyrs were substituted for the pagan gods and given their glory. In this way, pagan divinities continued in the Christian church with a thin veneer of a Christian name. When churches were built on the site of pagan temples, the old associations continued.

> The cult of the Virgin Diana may have contributed to the worship of the Virgin Mary and more than a coincidence may possibly be seen in the fact that one of the earliest churches in honour of Mary rose at Ephesus on the site of the famous Temple of Diana, and that in the same city in [AD] 431, a synod was held which first officially designated Mary the Mother of God.[113]

Remnants of magical beliefs were carried into the church. Christians in Gaul used the sign of the cross to protect their cattle against the plague. The name of the Trinity was pronounced over a magic drink. In some places, water was sprinkled on the faces of horses from the horn of St. Hilarion. Pagan use of amulets was substituted by using relics, portions of the Gospels, crosses, medals, and more. One could continue almost indefinitely with examples of syncretism not only in practice but in belief. Many of these practices sparked the re-examination of Scriptures, resulting in the Protestant Reformation with Martin Luther's posting of his *Ninety-five Theses* in AD 1517.

Industrial Revolution to Modern Day

The world view of Christian civilization in western cultures was drastically altered again during the Enlightenment (AD 1685–1815). During this time, philosophers turned away from Scripture and church authority declaring *reason* to be their ultimate source of knowledge. They rejected the supernatural (including miracles and prophecies), doubted the historicity of Jesus recorded in the Gospels, and accepted the naturalistic origins of the universe through the theory of evolution.

As theologians began accepting a naturalistic world view, they questioned the accuracy of the Bible. Prophecies were re-interpreted as history told as prophecies. Miracles were rejected. Numerous Protestant churches absorbed this world view shift and continue to be influenced by it still today.

SYNCRETISM IN AFRICAN CHRISTIAN THEOLOGY

Like their counterparts in the west, some theologians in Africa embrace the naturalistic world view. They no longer accept the Bible as God's infallible revelation. And in rejecting the unjust colonialization of Africa, they also reject the Christian faith brought by the western missionaries. They deconstruct western missionary theology and seek to unite, harmonise, or fuse together African traditions with Christian theology. What they create is something very different; it is neither African nor Christian, but an amalgamation of both, designing something new through their own imaginative creativity, the very definition of syncretism.

These theologians all admit the importance of Scripture, but they do not believe Scripture is *infallible* or *their final authority*. Itumeleng Mosala of South Africa believes that Black Theology cannot claim the whole Bible, for doing so ignores "the results of biblical scholarship over the last century and has its roots in ruling-class ideology."[114] Further, the words of Scripture cannot be taken at face value but must be reinterpreted ideologically. A survey of many theologians in Africa reveals their view of Scripture is neither biblical nor African but formed by western *un*belief.

The Future

Thankfully, there are a growing number of evangelical African believers who remain faithful to Scripture and are ardent in their love for Jesus Christ.

We firmly believe, despite ongoing temptations of syncretism, Christ's church will prevail.

Our prayer is that you find this basic outline of biblical teaching on the traditional beliefs and practices in Africa helpful in your own lives; that through the lens of Scripture, you will understand the truth and error in ATR, knowing that God "has not left himself without testimony" (Acts 14:17, NIV), "so that people are without excuse" (Romans 1:20, NIV). May you not be people who "suppress the truth" and whose "foolish hearts [are] darkened" (Romans 1:18, 21, NIV), but rather be the true followers Jesus described when he said, "You are truly my disciples if you remain faithful to my teachings. And you will know the truth, and the truth will set you free" (John 8:31).

Bibliography

Adeyemo, Tokunboh. *Salvation in African Tradition*. Nairobi: Evangel Publishing House, 1979.

Baxter, H. C. "Religious Practices of the Pagan Wazigua: The Story of a Dying Creed" in *Tanzania Notes and Records,* 15 (June 1943).

Booth, Newell S., ed. *African Religions: A Symposium*. NOK Publishers, 1977.

Budge, E. A. Wallis, ed. *The Egyptian Book of the Dead*. University Books, 1960.

Buttrick, George A., ed. *The Interpreter's Dictionary of the Bible*. Nashville: Abingdon Press, 1962.

Cory, Hans. "Religious Beliefs and Practices of the Sukuma/Nyamwezi Tribal Groups," in *Tanganyika Notes and Records*, 54 (March 1960).

Cullman, Oscar. *Christ and Time*. Philadelphia: The Westminster Press, 1964.

Douglas, J. D., ed. *The New Bible Dictionary*. Inter-Varsity Fellowship, 1962.

Dundas, Charles. *Kilimanjaro and Its People*. London: H. F. & G. Witherby, 1924.

Éla, Jean-Marc. *My Faith as an African*. Orbis Books, 1988.

Elwell, Walter A., ed. *Evangelical Dictionary of Theology*. Ada: Baker Books, 1984.

Evans-Pritchard, E. E. *Witchcraft, Oracles and Magic among the Azande*. Oxford: Oxford University Press, 1937.

Farquhar, J. N. *The Crown of Hinduism*. Oxford: Oxford University Press, 1913.

Ferdinando, Keith. *The Triumph of Christ in African Perspective*. Exeter: Paternoster Press, 1999.

Gehman, Richard J. *African Christian Theology Revisited*. Wheaton: Oasis International Ltd, 2018.

Gehman, Richard J. *African Traditional Religion in Biblical Perspective,* 1st edition. Kesho Publications, 1987.

Gehman, Richard J. *African Traditional Religion in Biblical Perspective*, 3rd edition. Wheaton: Oasis International Ltd., 2005.

Gehman, Richard J. *Overcoming Fear of Death*. Wheaton: Oasis International Ltd., 2017.

Glasswell, Mark and Edward Fasholé-Luke, eds. *New Testament Christianity for Africa and the World*. London: SPCK, 1974.

Grant, Earl. "Folk Religion in Islam." Unpublished PhD. Thesis. Pasadena: Fuller Theological Seminary, 1987.

Gulliver, P. H. "A Preliminary Survey of the Turkana," a report compiled for the Government of Kenya. University of Cape Town, mimeographed, 1951.

Hiebert, Paul. *Anthropological Reflections on Missiological Issues*. Ada: Baker, 1994.

Hiebert, Paul, D. Shaw & Tite Tiénou, *Understanding Folk Religion*. Ada: Baker, 1999.

Hughes, Langston. *An African Treasury*. Victor Gollancz Ltd., 1961.

Idowu, E. Bolaji. *Olodumare: God in Yoruba Belief*. London: Longmans, 1962.

James, E. O. *Prehistoric Religion: A Study in Prehistoric Archaeology*. New York: Barnes and Noble, Inc., 1962.

Johnston, Jerry. *The Edge of Evil: The Rise of Satanism in North America*. Nashville: W Publishing Group, 1989.

Kenyatta, Jomo. *Facing Mount Kenya: The Tribal Life of the Gikuyu*. New York: Vintage Books, 1965.

King, Noel Q. *African Cosmos: An Introduction to Religion in Africa*. Belmont: Wadsworth, 1986.

Langley, Sara Myrtle. *The Nandi of Kenya*. New York: St. Martin's, 1979.

Latourette, Kenneth S. *A History of the Expansion of Christianity*, Volume 1. New York: Harper, 1937.

Lewis, Gordon and Bruce Demarest. *Integrative Theology*, Volume 1. Grand Rapids: Zondervan, 1994.

Lindblom, Gerhard. *The Akamba*. Uppsala: Appelbergs, 1920.

Luzbetak, Louis. *The Church and Cultures: An Applied Anthropology for the Religious Worker*. Littleton: William Carey Library, 1976.

Mbiti, John. *African Religions and Philosophy*. London: SPCK, 1969.

Mbiti, John. *Concepts of God in Africa*. London: SPCK, 1969.

McClintock, John and James Strong, *Cyclopaedia of Biblical, Theological and Ecclesiastical Literature*. Ada: Baker, 1981.

Mosala, Itumeleng. *Biblical Hermeneutics and Black Theology in South Africa*. Grand Rapids: William. B. Eerdmans Publishing Company, 1989.

Mulago, Vincent. "Traditional African Religion and Christianity" in *African Traditional Religion in Contemporary Society*, edited by J. K. Olupona. New York: Paragon House, 1991.

Ndeti, Kivuto. *Elements of Akamba Life*. Nairobi: East African Publishing House, 1972.

Nevius, John. *Demon Possession*. Grand Rapids: Kregel Publications, 1968.

Nyamiti, Charles. "Ancestral Veneration and its Relevance to the African Churches," in *African Christian Studies*, Vol. 9 No. 3 (September 1993).

Nxumalo, J. A. "Zulu Christians and Ancestor Cult" in *Ancestor Religion in Southern Africa*. Pretoria: Lumko Missiological Institute, 1981.

Olowola, Cornelius. *African Traditional Religion and the Christian Faith*. Achimota: Africa Christian Press, 1993.

O'Neill, C. "Saints, Devotion to" in *New Catholic Encyclopedia*. Farmington Hills: Gale Publishing Group, 2003.

Opoku, Kofi Asare. *West African Traditional Religion*. Singapore: FEP International Private Ltd., 1978.

Orr, James ed. *The International Standard Bible Encyclopaedia*, Volume III. Grand Rapids: William. B. Eerdmans Publishing Company, 1952.

Parrinder, Geoffrey. *African Traditional Religion*. London: Sheldon Press, 1962.

Parrinder, Geoffrey. *West African Religion*. London: Epworth Press, 1961.

Parrinder, Geoffrey. *Witchcraft: European and African*. London: Faber & Faber, 1958.

Pope, Richard. *The Church and its Culture*. Bloomington: Bethany Press, 2003.

Quarcoopome, T. N. O. *West African Traditional Religion*. Ibadan: African Universities Press, 1987.

Roberts, Alexander and James Donaldson, eds. *The Ante-Nicene Fathers*, Volume 3. Grand Rapids: William. B. Eerdmans Publishing Company, 1963.

Salalah, Charles. "The Place of Ancestral Spirits in African Theology". Unpublished MA Thesis. Columbia Graduate School of Bible and Missions, 1981.

Sawyerr, Harry. *God: Ancestor or Creator? Aspects of Traditional Beliefs in Ghana, Nigeria, and Sierra Leone*. London: Longmans, 1970.

Smith, Edwin. *African Ideas of God*. London: Edinburgh House Press, 1966.

Summers, Montague. *The History of Witchcraft and Demonology*. Oxfordshire: Routledge, 1973.

Taylor, John. *The Primal Vision: Christian Presence amid African Religion*. London: SCM Press, 1963.

Tjandra, Lucas. "Folk Religion among the Chinese in Singapore and Malaysia." Unpublished DMiss. Dissertation. Pasadena: Fuller Theological Seminary, 1988.

Turaki, Yusufu. *Christianity and African Gods: A Method in Theology*. Potchefstroom: Potchefstroom University for Higher Education, 1999.

Unger, Merrill F. *The Haunting of Bishop Pike: A Christian View of the Other Side*. Carol Stream: Tyndale, 1971.

Unger, Merrill F. *Unger's Bible Dictionary*. Chicago: Moody Press, 1960.

Unger, Merrill F. *What Demons Can Do to Saints*. Chicago: Moody Press, 1977.

Warner, Timothy. "An Evangelical Position on Bondage and Exorcism" in *Essays on Spiritual Bondage and Deliverance*. Elkhart: Institute of Mennonite Studies, 1988.

Westermann, Diedrich. *Africa and Christianity*. Oxford: Oxford University Press, 1937.

Yamamori, Tetsunao and Charles Taber (eds.). *Christopaganism or Indigenous Christianity?* Littleton: William Carey Library, 1975.

Endnotes

1. Louis Luzbetak. *The Church and Cultures: An Applied Anthropology for the Religious Worker* (Littleton: William Carey Library, 1976), 59-64.
2. Gordon Lewis and Bruce Demarest. *Integrative Theology*, Volume 1 (Grand Rapids: Zondervan, 1994), 231-239.
3. Deity of Jesus: John 1:1-2, 14; 10:30-36; Philippians 2:5-8; Colossians 1:15-17; 2:9. Deity of Holy Spirit: John 14:16-17; Acts 5:3-4. Three Persons of Godhead mentioned together: Matthew 3:16-17; Matthew 28:19; 1 Corinthians 12:4-6; 2 Corinthians 13:14; Ephesians 4:4-6; 1 Peter 1:1-2.
4. 1.1.1 Confessions by Augustine.
5. John Mbiti, *African Religions and Philosophy* (London: SPCK, 1969), 1.
6. Ibid.,104.
7. Oscar Cullman, *Christ and Time*, translated by F. V. Filson (Philadelphia: The Westminster Press, 1964).
8. Sara Myrtle Langley, *The Nandi of Kenya* (*Life Crisis Rituals in a Period of Change*) (New York: St. Martin's, 1979), 115.
9. Mbiti, *African Religions and Philosophy*, 197.
10. Paul Hiebert, Daniel Shaw and Tite Tiénou, *Understanding Folk Religion* (Ada: Baker Books, 1999), 66.
11. Mbiti, *African Religions and Philosophy*, 199.
12. E. E. Evans-Pritchard, *Witchcraft, Oracles and Magic among the Azande*, abridged (Oxford: Oxford University Press, 1976), 176.
13. Jomo Kenyatta, *Facing Mount Kenya* (New York: Vintage Books, 1965), 294.
14. Geoffrey Parrinder, *Witchcraft: European and African* (London: Faber & Faber, 1958).
15. Jerry Johnston, *The Edge of Evil: The Rise of Satanism in North America* (Nashville: W Publishing Group, 1989).
16. Parrinder, *Witchcraft: European and African*, 166.
17. Montague Summers, *The History of Witchcraft and Demonology* (Oxfordshire: Routledge, 1973), 64.
18. Vincent Mulago, "Traditional African Religion and Christianity" in *African Traditional Religion in Contemporary Society*, edited by J. K. Olupona (New York: Paragon House, 1991), 13, 130.

19. John McClintock and James Strong. *Cyclopaedia of Biblical, Theological and Ecclesiastical Literature* (Ada: Baker, 1981), 827.
20. Evans-Pritchard, *Witchcraft, Oracles and Magic among the Azande.*
21. The Greek word is *pharmakeia* from which we derive the English word, "pharmacy" meaning "drug store." Clearly, this also refers to the use of herbs though the NLT reads "*participation in demonic activities.*"
22. The Hebrew word, *cheber*, is translated in the NLT, NIV, NASB and NEB by the words, "cast spells." The AV, RSV, and ESV translate it as "charmer," while the NEB uses "charms."
23. Paul Hiebert, *Anthropological Reflections on Missiological Issues* (Ada: Baker Books, 1994).
24. Diedrich Westermann, *Africa and Christianity* (Oxford: Oxford University Press, 1937), 75.
25. Keith Ferdinando, *The Triumph of Christ in African Perspective* (Exeter: Paternoster, 1999), 379.
26. Tokunbo Adeyemo, *Salvation in African Tradition* (Nairobi: Evangel Pub. House, 1979), 93.
27. Unknown, "Under the Blood of Jesus," cited by Grace Community Church (http://www.rvgrace.com/hymns/under_the_blood_of_jesus.htm: 2008); archived at *Wayback Machine* (https://web.archive.org/web/20130121233226/www.rvgrace.com/hymns/under_the_blood_of_jesus.htm); citing a capture dated 21 Jan 2013.
28. Richard J. Gehman, *African Christian Theology Revisited* (Wheaton: Oasis, 2018).
29. Kofi Asare Opoku, *West African Traditional Religion* (Singapore: FEP International Private Ltd., 1978), 14f.
30. Newell S. Booth, ed., *African Religions: A Symposium* (NOK Pub., 1977), 16.
31. Noel Q. King, *African Cosmos: An Introduction to Religion in Africa* (Belmont: Wadsworth, 1986), 10.
32. Opoku, op cit, 54.
33. T. N. O. Quarcoopome, *West African Traditional Religion* (Ibadan: African Universities Press, 1987), 70.
34. E. Bolaji Idowu, *Olodumare: God in Yoruba Belief* (London: Longmans, 1962), 142.
35. Booth, op. cit., 16.
36. Cornelius Olowola, *African Traditional Religion and the Christian Faith* (Achimota: Africa Christian Press, 1993), 43.

37. Ibid.
38. Ibid.
39. Yusufu Turaki, *Christianity and African Gods: A Method in Theology* (Potchefstrom University for Higher Education, 1999), 175f.
40. Olowola, *African Traditional Religion and the Christian Faith,* 45f.
41. Mbiti, *African Religions and Philosophy,* 25-27.
42. Ibid., 58.
43. Edwin Smith, *African Ideas of God* (London: Edinburgh House Press, 1966), 25.
44. Langston Hughes, *An African Treasury* (Victor Gollancz, 1961), 184f.
45. Wallis E. A. Budge, ed. *The Egyptian Book of the Dead* (University Books, 1960).
46. For a greater depth of African traditional beliefs the reader should consult other textbooks on ATR, including *African Traditional Religion in Biblical Perspective* by Richard J. Gehman (Wheaton: Oasis, 2005).
47. 1 Chronicles 21:1; Job 1–2; Psalm 109:6; Zechariah 3:1, 2.
48. The English word, *shade* derived from the Hebrew Word, *shed,* refers to comparative darkness as one sheltered from the sun. *Shade* in English can also refer to a ghost, the spirit of the dead residing in darkness of shade.
49. The King James (Authorized Version) calls her "a woman that hath a familiar spirit." A more appropriate translation, followed by modern translations, calls her a "medium."
50. Alexander Roberts and James Donaldson, eds. *The Ante-Nicene Fathers,* Vol. 3 (Grand Rapids: William B. Eerdmans Pub. Co., 1963), 234.
51. "idols" translates '*ililim* from the Hebrew, meaning "of nought, worthless, vain"; translated into the Greek (Septuagint Greek version), *daimonia*, or demons.
52. Olowola, *African Traditional Religion and the Christian Faith*, 30.
53. *Merriam-Webster.com Thesaurus*, s.v. "spiritist," accessed September 5, 2023, https://www.merriam-webster.com/thesaurus/spiritist.
54. Adapted from *African Traditional Religion in Biblical Perspective*, first edition, by Richard J. Gehman (Kijabe: Kesho Publications, 1987), 267-286.
55. Richard Pope, *The Church and its Culture* (Bloomington: Bethany Press, 2003), 148f.

56. C. O'Neill, "Saints, Devotion to," in *New Catholic Encyclopedia* 2nd ed. (Farmington Hills: Gale Publishing Group, 2003), 597.
57. William G. Most, "The Catholic Church is the Mystical Body of Christ" (EWTN.com, 1990), accessed September 29, 2023 https://www.ewtn.com/catholicism/teachings/catholic-church-is-the-mystical-body-of-christ-89.
58. Charles Nyamiti, "Ancestral Veneration and its Relevance to the African Churches," *African Christian Studies*, Vol. 9 No. 3 (September 1993), 17.
59. J. A. Nxumalo, "Zulu Christians and Ancestor Cult – A Personal Consideration," in *Ancestor Religion in Southern Africa: Proceedings of a Seminar on Ancestor Belief* (Lumko Missiological Institute, 1981), 69.
60. Jean-Marc Éla, *My Faith as an African* (Orbis Books, 1988), 31 & 18.
61. John Taylor, *The Primal Vision: Christian Presence Amid African Religion* (London: SCM Ltd., 1963), 160.
62. Mark Glasswell and Edward Fasholé-Luke, eds. *New Testament Christianity for Africa and the World* (SPCK, 1974), 210.
63. Ibid., 217.
64. Daidanso ma Djongwe, former Assistant General Secretory of the Association of Evangelicals of Africa, personal interview, 1988.
65. Merrill F. Unger, *The Haunting of Bishop Pike: A Christian View of the Other Side* (Carol Stream: Tyndale, 1971), 102.
66. Merrill F. Unger, *What Demons Can Do to Saints* (Chicago: Moody Press, 1977), 87.
67. Timothy Warner, "An Evangelical Position on Bondage and Exorcism," in *Essays on Spiritual Bondage and Deliverance* (Elkhart: Institute of Mennonite Studies, 1988), 86.
68. John Nevius, *Demon Possession* (Grand Rapids: Kregel Publications, 1968).
69. Gerhard Lindblom, *The Akamba* (Uppsala: Appelbergs, 1920), 216.
70. Kivuto Ndeti, *Elements of Akamba Life* (Nairobi: East African Pub. House, 1972), 175.
71. Geoffrey Parrinder, *West African Religion* (London: Epworth Press, 1961), 18.
72. James 1:17.
73. *Merriam-Webster.com Dictionary*, s.v. "worship," accessed September 6, 2023, https://www.merriam-webster.com/dictionary/worship.

74. John Mbiti, *Concepts of God in Africa* (London: SPCK, 1969), 178.
75. E. O. James, *Prehistoric Religion: A Study in Prehistoric Archaeology* (New York: Barnes & Noble, 1962), 206-207.
76. J. N. Farquhar, *The Crown of Hinduism* (Oxford: Oxford University Press, 1913), 71.
77. Lucas Tjandra, "Folk Religion among the Chinese in Singapore and Malaysia." Unpublished DMiss. Dissertation. Fuller Theological Seminary, 1988, 54.
78. Earl Grant, "Folk Religion in Islam" (PhD Thesis, Fuller Theological Seminary, 1987).
79. Yusufu Turaki, *Christianity and African Gods: A Method in Theology* (Potchefstrom University for Higher Education, 1999), 28.
80. See Kofi Asare Opoku, *West African Traditional Religion* (14-18) and John Mbiti, *Concepts of God in Africa* (Praeger Publishers, 1970).
81. Mbiti, *Concepts of God in Africa*, 23.
82. Reginald Heber, "From Greenland's Icy Mountains," (1918), as cited on *Hymnary.org* (https://hymnary.org/text/from_greenlands_icy_mountains), accessed 7 September, 2023.
83. George A. Buttrick, ed., *The Interpreter's Dictionary of the Bible* (Abingdon Press, 1962), 675.
84. J. D. Douglas, ed., *The New Bible Dictionary* (Inter-Varsity Fellowship, 1962), 553.
85. Merrill Unger, *Unger's Bible Dictionary* (Chicago: Moody Press, 1960), 512.
86. James Orr, ed., *The International Standard Bible Encyclopaedia*, Vol. III (Grand Rapids: William B. Eerdmans Pub. Co., 1952), 1448.
87. Jomo Kenyatta, *Facing Mount Kenya: The Tribal Life of the Gikuyu* (New York: Vintage Books, 1965), 225.
88. Ibid., 225.
89. Ibid., 227.
90. P. H. Gulliver, "A Preliminary Survey of the Turkana," a report compiled for the Government of Kenya, University of Cape Town, mimeographed, 1951, 230.
91. H. C. Baxter, "Religious Practices of the Pagan Wazigua: The Story of a Dying Creed," *Tanzania Notes and Records*, 15 (June 1943), 4.

92. Charles Dundas, *Kilimanjaro and Its People* (London: H. F. & G. Witherby, 1924), 107.
93. Hans Cory, "Religious Beliefs and Practices of the Sukuma/Nyamwezi Tribal Group," *Tanganyika Notes and Records*, 54 (March 1960), 15.
94. Geoffrey Parrinder, *African Traditional Religion* (London: Sheldon Press, 1962), 38.
95. Taylor, *The Primal Vision*, 79.
96. Ibid., 78.
97. Ibid., 76.
98. Mbiti, *Concepts of God in Africa*, 18.
99. Mbiti, *African Religions and Philosophy*, 35.
100. Harry Sawyerr, *God: Ancestor or Creator? Aspects of Traditional Beliefs in Ghana, Nigeria, and Sierra Leone* (London: Longmans, 1970), 6.
101. Ibid., 7.
102. Taylor, *The Primal Vision,* 80.
103. Smith, *African Ideas of God,* 186f.
104. Ndeti, *Elements of Akamba Life*, 174.
105. Charles Salalah, "The Place of Ancestral Sprits in African Theology: Evaluated in the Biblical Teaching." Unpublished MA Thesis. Columbia Graduate School of Bible and Missions, 1981), 53.
106. Ibid., 61.
107. Personal interview with Aaron Itumbuthi.
108. Richard Gehman, *African Christian Theology Revisited* (Wheaton: Oasis International, 2018).
109. Adeyemo, *Salvation in African Tradition*, 93.
110. Walter A. Elwell, ed., *Evangelical Dictionary of Theology* (Ada: Baker, 1984), 1062.
111. Yamamori, Tetsunao and Charles Taber (eds.), *Christopaganism or Indigenous Christianity?* (Littleton: William Carey Library, 1975), 17.
112. Kenneth Scott Latourette, *A History of the Expansion of Christianity*, Volume 1 (New York: Harper, 1937), p. 319.
113. Ibid., 320.
114. Itumeleng Mosala, *Biblical Hermeneutics and Black Theology in South Africa* (Grand Rapids: William B. Eerdmans, 1989), 16.

Resources for Pastors

There are many resources which can equip your leading and ministry, including some which have been created in Africa for our contexts. Oasis recommends:

ESSENTIAL LEADERSHIP LESSONS
Richard J. Gehman
Essential Leadership Lessons covers topics of leadership, love, essentials, humility, holiness, attributes, and management skills. While the context and application of these leadership lessons were created with the people of Africa in mind, the principles of Christian leadership are the same everywhere, for everyone, on all continents.

THE DISCIPLER'S TOOLKIT
George M. Mutuku and Mark A. Olander
The churches in Sub-Saharan Africa are growing numerically, primarily through evangelism. But evangelism is only the beginning of the disciple making process. This book takes people step by step from evangelism to establishing new believers in the faith, equipping them in spiritual disciplines and gifts, and sending them out to engage the world with the gospel.

THE MULTI-CHURCH PASTOR
Philip E. Morrison
The Multi-Church Pastor will help pastors solve the unique and complex issues of leading more than one congregation by teaching them, step-by-step, how to raise up the elders in their churches to lead with them. These skills can be applied by pastors whether or not they have formal ministerial training.

HELPING WITHOUT HURTING IN AFRICA
Jonny Kabiswa Kyazze and Anthony Sytsma with Brian Fikkert
This book trains leaders to proclaim the gospel in both word and deed, changing mind-sets and helping them apply biblical principles to care wisely and compassionately for people who are poor without unintentionally doing harm.

SOLVING CORRUPTION IN THE CHURCH AND NATION
Richard J. Gehman
A major problem is that in practice the Christian church so often reflects the same moral rot found in society. The church has failed to be salt and light. *Solving Corruption in the Church and Nation* shines light on this problem and explores a biblical solution. This book is for you because it points to the solution for this ongoing and unending moral mess.

CONFLICT RESOLUTION IN THE CHURCH
Philip Morrison with Chris Mwalw'a
This book is an answer to the great need the church has for a practical approach to conflict resolution in the church. It focuses on scripturally-based, peace-making attitudes within the African church context.

OASIS INTERNATIONAL PUBLISHING

oasisinternationalpublishing.com | oasisinternational.com

AFRICAN TRADITIONAL RELIGION AND CHRISTIAN COUNSELING
Karl Grebe & Wilfred Fon
African Traditional Religion and Christian Counseling analyzes the African worldview, interprets it from a biblical perspective, and applies the insights into ministry.

SHARING THE GOSPEL WITH MUSLIMS
John Gilchrist
Gilchrist teaches us to seek common ground as we learn about our Muslim neighbours. Filled with hundreds of passages from the Bible and the Qur'an that compare and contrast Christian and Muslim beliefts.

BIBLICAL CHRISTIANITY IN AFRICAN PERSPECTIVE
Wilbur O'Donovan
This book is a survey of the major truths of the Christian faith as seen from the perspective of the African world view. Unlike most theology books, this book has been purposely written in readable everyday language, including many true African stories.

AFRICAN TRADITIONAL RELIGION IN BIBLICAL PERSPECTIVE
Richard J. Gehman
Seeking to evaluate African traditional religion in biblical perspective, this book is a must-have for pastors and Bible students. It explores the issues of the supreme being, divinities, ancestral spirits, witchcraft, and sorcery in the light of God's Word.

AIDS IS REAL AND IT'S IN OUR CHURCH
Jean Garland and Mike Blyth
AIDS is Real and it's in our Church features information about AIDS in Africa, how to prevent HIV infection, and encouragement towards a Christian response to the AIDS epidemic.

AFRICAN CHRISTIAN THEOLOGY REVISITED
Richard J. Gehman
For all African Christians, *African Christian Theology Revisited* is a powerful plea to think through your faith in African contexts under the authority of the Word of God.

OASIS INTERNATIONAL PUBLISHING

oasisinternationalpublishing.com | oasisinternational.com

OASIS INTERNATIONAL

Satisfying Africa's Thirst for God's Word

Our mission is to grow discipleship through publishing African voices.
Go to oasisinternationalpublishing.com to learn more.

INFLUENCE: LEADING WITHOUT POSITION
Philip E. Morrison & Hankuri Tawus Gaya
Do you have ideas for how to change your community, church, or nation – but feel powerless to make them happen? This book tells you how you can influence others to take action and start change, just as young men and women in the Bible did.

HIGHLY FAVOURED: OUR POWERFUL GOD'S COVENANT WITH YOU
Stuart J. Foster
The God of the Bible is not unreliable or inaccessible like the spiritual beings in African traditional religions. He chooses to have a covenant relationship with his people and we do not have to earn God's favour.

THE SISTERHOOD SECRET
Levina Mulandi
In this book, Dr Mulandi shows how discipling is more than Bible study or a church program. She shares how she empowers any woman to mentor younger women, guiding them to understand their identity, discern the purpose of their lives, and be transformed to be more like Christ.

BAESICS
Ernest Wamboye with Waturi Wamboye
In *Baesics*, Ernest and Waturi Wamboye give no-nonsense advice on how to build a fulfilling love life and marriage. Young adults in African cities feel marriage is priority but are often unprepared. *Baesics* addresses the relationship dilemmas many young adults are facing today from a Christian point of view.

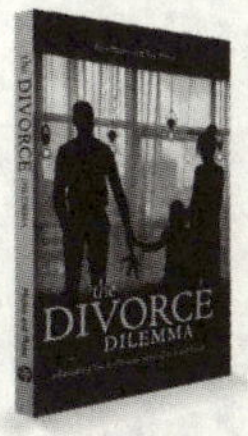

THE DIVORCE DILEMMA
Ron Misiko & Ray Motsi
The authors share their experiences as pastors and as married people, as well as their areas of expertise in the legal system and Bible scholarship. From their different African contexts, they explain how to navigate the challenges we face today with biblical and practical solutions for divorce care in African churches.

A PRE-MARRIAGE COUNSELLING HANDBOOK
Alan & Donna Goerz
This handbook was written specifically for the African context on how to build a successful marriage. Designed as a seminar-in-a-book, *A Pre-Marriage Counselling Handbook* equips pastors and counselors to teach biblical pre-marriage classes and seminars.

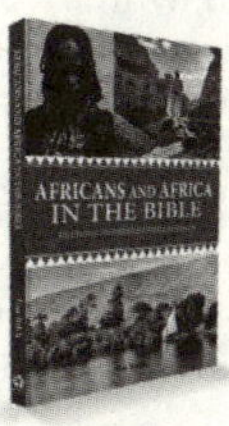

AFRICANS AND AFRICA IN THE BIBLE
Tim Welch
This book shows the presence and the participation of Africans in the biblical text, helping demonstrate that Christianity is not a "white man's religion" and that Christianity has deep roots in African soil.

ANSWERS FOR YOUR MARRIAGE
Bruce and Carol Britten
Offers practical insights to marriage issues and facts on sex, pregnancy, family planning, child-raising, money issues, adultery, HIV, and sex-related diseases. If your marriage is in despair, look to this book for some answers for your marriage.

PARENTING WITH PURPOSE & AFRICAN WISDOM
Gladys K. Mwiti
This practical guide for Christians is a relevant, thoughtful presentation on the characteristics of parenting that delivers results.

A WITNESS FOR EVER
Michael Cassidy
Michael Cassidy reveals for the first time what went on behind the scenes, away from the dramatic headlines, as South Africa inched its way towards the momentous election. Learn the first-hand account of the miracles that led to a peaceful end of apartheid in South Africa.

OASIS INTERNATIONAL PUBLISHING

oasisinternationalpublishing.com | oasisinternational.com

AFRICA STUDY BIBLE, NLT

God's Word Through African Eyes

The *Africa Study Bible* is the most ethnically-diverse, single-volume, biblical resource to date. Written by 350 contributors from 50 countries, it includes the Holy Bible: New Living Translation, and more than 2,600 features that illuminate the truth of Scripture with a unique, African perspective.

The *Africa Study Bible* is a monumental study Bible, with notes by scholars and pastors in Africa who see the critical need to make Scripture relevant to our everyday lives. It's an all-in-one course in biblical content, theology, history, and culture.

"The Africa Study Bible *is a model of contextualized engagement of the Scriptures, with notes written by Africans, written for Africans, and answers Bible questions asked in African cultural contexts. It's a great encouragement to me to see such a resource available and I recommend it widely!"*
- Dr Ed Stetzer, Executive Director of the BILLY GRAHAM CENTER

Discover more at ***africastudybible.com***

DOWNLOAD THE
***AFRICA STUDY BIBLE* APP**

The Africa Study Bible app is now on the Tecarta Bible App, the world's best study Bible app which is available to download on Google Play Store and Apple App Store.

Download on the App Store

GET IT ON Google Play

SATISFYING AFRICA'S THIRST FOR GOD'S WORD

OASIS INTERNATIONAL
is devoted to growing discipleship
through publishing African voices.

Engaging Africa's most influential,
most relevant, and best communicators for the sake of the gospel.

Creating contextual content that meets the specific needs of Africa,
has the power to transform individuals and societies, and gives the
church in Africa a global voice.

Cultivating local and global partnerships in order to publish
and distribute high-quality books and Bibles.

Visit **oasisinternational.com** to learn more about our vision,
for Africa to equip its own leaders to impact the global church.

OASIS INTERNATIONAL
oasisinternational.com

OASIS INTERNATIONAL PUBLISHING
oasisinternationalpublishing.com

GOD'S WORD FOR AFRICA
godswordforafrica.com